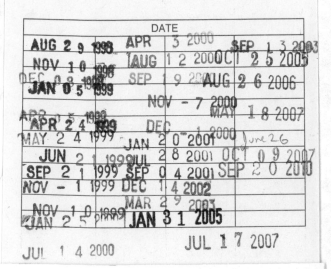

250 Things

You Can Do

to Make Your Cat

Adore You

Ingrid Newkirk

A FIRESIDE BOOK
Published by Simon & Schuster

F

FIRESIDE
Rockefeller Center
1230 Avenue of the Americas
New York, NY 10020

FIRESIDE and colophon are registered trademarks of Simon & Schuster Inc.

Designed by Kathryn Parise

Manufactured in the United States of America

1   3   5   7   9   10   8   6   4   2

LIBRARY OF CONGRESS CATALOGING-IN-PUBLICATION DATA
NEWKIRK, INGRID.
250 THINGS YOU CAN DO TO MAKE YOUR CAT ADORE YOU / INGRID NEWKIRK.
P.   CM.
"A FIRESIDE BOOK."
INCLUDES BIBLIOGRAPHICAL REFERENCES.
1. CATS. I. TITLE.
SF447.N49   1998
636.8' 083—DC21   97-52060 CIP
ISBN 0-684-83648-3

Acknowledgments

A cat book wouldn't be possible without cats, so the first big thank you goes to all the cats who have brought me joy and taught me important things about themselves.

I am also very grateful to Patti Breitman, not only for her professionalism, but also for her kindness.

Thanks, too, to present and past PETA staff members Alisa Mullins, Karen Porreca, Karen Johnson, Alison Green, Lisa Lange, Danielle Moore, Mindy Gregg, Bobbi Hoffman, and Carla and Karen Bennett, as well as to all those people who shared their cat experiences with me, including my parents and Maria Peterson (who has created the most cat-respectful private home I have ever visited).

Finally, thanks to the companies and individuals responsible for all the goodies, from wisdom to toys, that help us make cats absolutely adore us.

Contents

What Will This Book Do for Me and My Cat?

This book, *250 Things You Can Do to Make Your Cat Adore You,* has two simple but important goals: To make your cat happier and, as a result, to make you happier, too.

Over the years, I have shared ordinary, extraordinary, happy, and heartbreaking experiences with cats. The pointers I've picked up should be as useful to you as they have been to me, from tiny tips, such as which scratching posts are most likely to save the sofa from being shredded, to big ones such as how to find a cat who has suddenly vanished.

This book is written from the cat's perspective. Cats, like us, want to be comfortable, loved, stimulated, and fulfilled. They dislike being uncomfortable, lonely, bored, and frustrated. That's obvious enough, unless the reader is the experimenter I met long ago in a Maryland laboratory. Dr. Whatever-His-Name-Was called me "anthropomorphic" when I suggested that an enormous baboon, roughly the size of a football player and kept in a cage that fit snugly around his ears, would appreciate having enough room to be able to take a step!

Anthropomorphism is a silly, old-fashioned word. Even old Dr. Whatever from the baboon lab would probably be too embarrassed to bandy it about these days, although, in the past, everyone from hog butchers to people who practiced pigeon bowling (yes, it's just what it sounds like!), drowned kittens in a sack, or knocked giraffes unconscious to measure the thickness of their ears used "the A word" to convince bleeding hearts that cats and other animals do not experience "human" feelings like pain—a recognition that might have stayed the hand that carried kitty to the well or liverwurst to the lips.

Today, most of us have watched enough *National Geographic* specials to realize that we are *all* members of the animal kingdom, and that joy, fear, love, and amusement are not exclusively felt by Homo sapiens.

Some of my best lessons came from a cat named Moomin. When I first took her in, Moomin was a tiny, frail Siamese kitten with a respiratory virus that left her with a wheeze you could hear a mile away. She arrived at a time when cats were swarming about my house like June bugs. However, this tiny kitten was instantly drawn to the only other Siamese on the premises. Jarvis was very handsome, but reserved—to the point of snobbishness.

I doubt Moomin realized that she, too, was Siamese. I think she was drawn to Jarvis because he looked just like Mom and Dad. This lonely little kitten pursued Jarvis relentlessly. Every time she pulled her tiny wheezing body up to his, Jarvis swatted her across the face, spat, and made for higher ground. Yet, no matter how often he moved, no sooner had he settled down again than along came Moomin, squashing herself right up against him, certain that, at any moment, Jarvis would recognize her as "family."

After about a week, Jarvis gave up. He began to let Moomin sit beside him while still ignoring her. After a few weeks, I caught him grooming her. One day, the two of them became one. They did everything together: ate, slept, and once, in a fabulous feat of coordination, simultaneously threw up on my shoe.

After Jarvis died fourteen years later, Moomin spent weeks walking the house at night, crying for her lost love. Jarvis and Moomin's relationship taught me something quite obvious but important: Togetherness is a wonderful treasure—for cats as much as for people.

Togetherness does not mean ownership. "Own" is a word that doesn't work when it comes to cats, and not just because they are such independent animals. "Own" is a word that describes something like one's relationship to a VCR, but the idea of animals as possessions makes anyone who truly respects animals flinch.

Sure, this book is mainly about how to create unbridled happiness in your cat, but I'll have missed my mark if it does not also make you think about your relationship with all animals. This book will show you how to treat them, not as things, but as individuals.

By now I have given you an inkling that, in this book, from time to time, you will encounter the sort of pain-in-the-neck PETA philosophy that demands recognition for the idea that cats and, for that matter, all living beings, regardless of species, gender, size, or familiarity, have an inherent right to be treated with respect, even when they noisily bring up a hairball during a dinner party.

Don't worry. You don't have to envision life without baby back ribs or appreciate the tactics of people who jump up and down dressed as giant minks to get their point across to find the tips on these pages both practical and enriching. If you have a cat, or are contemplating sharing your life with one, this book is for you.

Everyone can be a terrific cat steward. Lots of people already do a good job in that role, but want to know more. Others care *about* cats but may not have a clue how to care *for* them. Even in the homes of dyed-in-the-wool cat lovers, I've met cats who were literally screaming for the right kind of attention and cats who had thrown in the towel and become as withdrawn as caterpillar grubs, *and their people didn't notice there was a problem!*

Although animal rights activists have been accused of worshiping cats and other animals, the truth is we don't. However, some of us, like me, do occasionally wonder if cats belong to a superior species. I mean, look at them. They are far more reliable, better behaved, more attentive, and much cleaner than most human beings. I'm sure the condition of my house sometimes scandalizes my cat. Especially when I'm working late and the whole place starts looking like a garage sale in progress.

Look at your cat. As if expecting visitors, your cat is always up in the morning, looking well rested, washed, and groomed. At mealtimes, you never have to shout, "For the umpteenth time, will you come and eat?" Cats are fastidious about their litter boxes, they try to keep their claws filed down, and they never snore.

Miraculously, despite this evidence of their superiority and our numerous shortcomings, cats seem to find us endearing or, at least, amusing. They are rarely critical and, if we're very good (or really pathetic), they may deign to snuggle up to us, a sensation as delightful to a "cat person" as a dip in a pool on a hot summer day. There are ways to shamelessly capitalize on this feline bonhomie and the fact that a cat, being of a polite and grateful nature, will give credit where credit is due. Which means that when you apply the advice herein, your cat will not just love you despite your inadequacies, but admire (yes, admire!) and even worship you.

Perhaps there is no greater proof of how "human" the other animals are than the realization that they can even lie! Take the true story of one young American Sign Language–taught chimpanzee who accidentally broke a toy. Not realizing he was being observed through the one-way glass, he decided to cover up his role in the mishap. When his teacher entered the room to ask, "Did you break the toy?" the guilty baby shook his head vigorously, pointed to another chimpanzee baby, and signed, "No. *He* did!"

Come to think of it, it's a wonder they have anything at all to do with us considering the bizarre impositions we have placed upon them throughout history. Remember, we have thrown cats aboard ships to act as unpaid rat catchers on perilous ocean voyages and buried them alive in tombs as favored possessions. Perhaps our ancestors were too busy trying to invent central heating and stud poker to treat cats with the respect they deserved, but that's no excuse for burning them at the stake (as they did in Salem and other places during the witch hunts!), tying their tails together to make them fight (a great eighteenth-century sport that people brought their knitting to), or, as was done in Europe, celebrating St. John's Day by sewing cats into sacks or wicker baskets.

Our behavior today isn't that hot either. In hundreds of laboratories, cats are still treated like test tubes with tails, and there are millions of abandoned strays scrounging through trash cans looking for sustenance and often finding only the cold and moldy leftovers of someone's dinner.

Caring about cats as you do makes you a very special person, perhaps far more special than you realize. Your cat is very lucky to have you. In fact, I wish all cats were so lucky. Not everyone has your level of commitment.

Visit your local animal shelter, and you will find it bursting at the seams with cast-off cats. Wonderful, well-behaved, attractive cats are waiting for you. Those cats didn't wake up one day and decide to play Russian roulette with their lives. They woke up one day to find their beloved family had decided to give them the old heave-ho. Humans can be incredibly cavalier about their obligations. When cats get old, sick, or inconvenient, more than a few people dispose of them or replace them with shiny, new cats as if these dear souls were of no more importance than used light bulbs.

Well, whatever your outlook, if you follow the suggestions on these pages, you should be really pleased with the results. Adoring eyes will follow you wherever you go. And the purring may get so loud you will have to buy earplugs. You will feel like a movie star.

What greater reward could anyone who loves cats hope for?

1

Home, Sweet Home

Or, is it? Could it be that your cat is living only one of her nine lives in a human-oriented dwelling place, and worse, living at ground level? Let me elaborate: Before cats belonged to human beings, they belonged to themselves. They answered to no one unless they felt like it. In fact, before fourteen-wheelers and human beings got into the act, cats had no natural enemies to speak of, except parasites, and even then, they knew which plants to chew on to fight off illness and even managed to pass on their folk remedies to their youngsters.

Yes, cats used to be self-sufficient in those halcyon days before we, if I may borrow Joni Mitchell's lyrics, paved their paradise and put up a parking lot. Cats also got along perfectly well, thank you very much, without can openers and litter boxes. Sure, they probably wouldn't have said no to a catnip toy, but their lives were full without such artificial stimulants.

They were whole, dignified, free-roaming, independent souls. They carved out their own, often vast, patches of turf, defended them with their own spit and claws, enjoyed a social life with friends and family, had the opportunity to flirt and to select and reject suitors, raised the kids, provided balanced meals for their families without benefit of advice from nutrition experts, and still had time to play "pounce." We humans were about as necessary to their existence as a bowling ball.

Now look at modern kitty's confines. Your cat is probably stuck inside a wood and cement box with compartments— otherwise known as your home.

Before you protest, "But *I* live there, too," chances are you leave your house or apartment every day. Sometimes you are in and out of the door so fast that your cat's image of you amounts to a big blur. Sometimes you are out and about so much, your cat can't remember what you look like.

Out in the real world, you see things your cat would give an eye tooth to see. You interact with others of your own kind, even if that only means swearing at the driver in front of you who brakes for falling leaves. Your brain and body are actively engaged, whether it's greeting neighbors and friends, running for the bus, drafting a memo, or making change.

Meanwhile, your cat is probably back home, staring at the wall. At least your cat *should* be indoors, unless you are conducting supervised leisure or exercise time, because today's outside world is a dangerous place for a cat, full of traffic and strangers with candy in their pockets who want to take your cat for a little ride (see chapter 10). This means your cat is virtually a shut-in! Your home is his entire world.

Take a look around Cat World. Unless you live somewhere like the Hearst Castle, there's probably not much to it from a cat's perspective. This calls for action! You have to fool Kittums into thinking you live in the most interesting place on Earth. You have to enrich his otherwise drab little life.

2

A Room with a View

First and foremost, whether you have spacious gardens or a squinty little view of a junkyard outside your window, cats MUST have comfy places to sit and look out. To the dedicated bird-watcher, nothing makes the time pass quicker, and the whiskers twitch faster, than the object of her natural, abiding interest and careful study.

While outwardly cats may appear aloof, just below the surface they are like that nosey neighbor in *Bewitched*. Provided with a view, your cat will not only have something to distract her from resenting your absence, but may actually figure out exactly who that handsome man is who visits the house up the street!

Ordinary windowsills are usually too small to accommodate even svelte feline bottoms. A cat likes to survey her domain while stretching or lounging and does not like to be seen wobbling about while moving from one strategic lookout point to another. Most cats don't give a hoot that

Brooke Shields can fit through those suicide-proof hotel windows. As they age, they tend to model themselves after Renoir's women or Chubby Checker. Skinny windowsills just won't do.

HOME IMPROVEMENTS

1

THE BEST FIX

Bob Walker, a San Diego architect, has shown the way, by incorporating a 110-foot (yup) carpeted, elevated catwalk into his house. If you don't look up, Bob's house could seem normal, but if you do, wow! The catwalk winds its way through several rooms at cat-perfect, near-ceiling height. It incorporates resting boxes, curving staircases to run up and down, peekaboo cutouts into cupboards and adjoining rooms, and more. The cats watch everything from up there, including the Walkers, their dog, and TV. Yes, cat fur floats down so the vacuum doesn't have to be taken up.

Walker's cat-friendly house, which took him and his wife, Frances Mooney, ten years to perfect, is very fancy. However, the less artistic among us can certainly make more modest constructions that will please felines to no end. The Walker house, by the way, can be visited in person (tour ticket proceeds benefit the National Cat Protection Society) or on the World Wide Web at www.thecatshouse.com. *Highly* recommended.

LESSER MEASURES

Get out your band saw or call a carpenter and replace that tightrope job with a windowsill at least one foot wide. Cover this renovation with two-inch foam rubber, then add soft but thick cushioning (nail it down so it doesn't move around or fall off), a thick piece of padded (of course) carpeting, or if you subscribe to *Architectural Digest* or *Better Homes and Gardens*, material that matches or complements your curtains.

Or, go shopping. Try a window perch, an easy-to-install plastic frame covered with faux sheepskin that hooks onto the windowsill. Available from Flexi-Mat Corporation, 2244 South Western Avenue, Chicago, IL 60608, (773-376-5500) or in department stores for about twenty dollars.

If your cat is already a bit of a blimp, you may need to install a ramp up to the ledge or platform. Otherwise, strategically placed furniture can do the trick.

THE EASIEST SOLUTION

Drag a bureau, bookcase or other solid bit of furniture over to the window and firmly attach to it a padded seat, e.g., a cushion or covered foam, to create hours of viewing pleasure.

CAT TREE

Buy a cat tree like the large catnip variety from FELIX (206-547-0042) or build the one pictured here. A tree is particularly satisfying because, of course, before cats were deprived of their real, natural lives, they lived and lazed about in trees and, to this day, carry a tree-lounging gene. Make sure your faux tree is positioned close enough to the window and in such a way as to allow kitty a dignified posture and a good view without causing her any eye or neck strain.

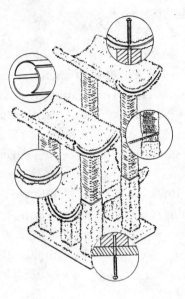

For Extra Credit

- The more scenic viewing spots the better. Windows are "cat TV," and if there's nothing playing on one channel, it's nice to have another to switch to.
- Place a bird feeder near the window in winter and spring (birds should not be fed year 'round; to do so foils their ability to forage).
- Try to catch the sun by providing at least one east- or west-facing "cat-bird seat." Cats long to sunbathe all year long!
- Oh, and if Tiddles is occupying a dining room chair at dinner time, or your favorite lounger during prime time, you wouldn't be so mean as to move him, would you? I thought not. Thank you.

Litterbox Alert

As you would wish to find it: That's how a cat's litterbox should always be left. Of all the indignities cats suffer at our hands, having us in charge of their litterbox arrangements is one of the worst. Cats' noses are sensitive, and their urine can be pungent. They do not wish to soil their dainty feet in it. Removing solid waste once or twice a day, or even after the act, isn't enough. A truly happy cat never has to wrinkle his nose—the litter pan is completely dumped out *daily*, swilled with vinegar, washed with soap, and then thoroughly rinsed and dried. Sometimes a little baking soda is placed under the litter. In multi-cat households, there is no less than one pan per two cats. Oh, how sweet life can be!

TOP TIP: Never use a pine-based cleaner. It can be toxic to cats. And as tempting as "clumping" litters may be, you should know that some experts think they may be doing to kitty's innards what they do to household plumbing—blocking it up. Writer Marina McInnis relates how three kittens deteriorated from "a robust, healthy group" to "thin, dehydrated little skeletons" with claylike bowel movements, which had the consistency of the clumping litter they were using. The stools even had gray and blue flecks inside them, just as with the litter itself, and smelled of clay. She says that only emergency medical care, in this case a holistic treatment that included slippery elm bark and lots of broth, saved them.

Holistic health practitioner, Lisa Newman, adds to the evidence. In "Healthy Pets—Naturally" (April 1994), Newman wrote, "There has been a rise in depressed immune systems, respiratory distress, irritable bowel syndrome, and vomiting (other than hair balls), among cats I have seen in the past two years. All had one thing in common—a clumping product in their litterboxes. In several cases, simply removing the litter improved the condition of the cat."

To be absolutely sure that your cats' litter is free of chemical deodorizers and other stuff, you can use alfalfa-based litters, which may be hard to find, or natural clay types, which use chlorophyll. Whatever you do, change their litter and clean the box no less than once a day. There you have it.

HOME HAZARDS

A home should also be a haven, not a place where a cat needs a hard hat and steel-toed boots. Check your place for these hazards:

1. Electrical cords. Unplug anything heavy that could topple over and injure a playful cat or kitten who decides to play with the cord.

2. Recliner chairs and fold-a-beds. Cats like dark places and beds and find them perfect for hiding out or pondering their navels. Cats who are caught in the mechanism when the chair or bed is opened or closed can be seriously injured or killed.

3. The dryer. Always check your dryer before turning it on (see chapter 15).

4. Cords. Cats love to play with curtain and blind cords, but they can easily get all wrapped up in them and strangle. Coil the cords up to the top of the window and pin them there with a clothes pin.

5. Bags with handles. Cats can become stuck in the handles and panic. If this happens when you are not home, the cat may be injured or killed. Keep such bags out of reach of the cats, or cut handles off.

6. Stove tops. Gas or electrical stoves can present problems. Use burner covers. Most cats will stay away from anything actively hot, but you may wish to train them away from the stove by spraying them with a little water.

7. Conventional antifreeze, which contains ethylene glycol, is poisonous. Just one teaspoon can kill a cat. Antifreeze should never be left lying around, but for extra safety buy Sierra, which is less toxic and made with animals in mind. It is available from automotive product retailers or call 1-800-289-7234.

3

A Mind Is a Terrible
Thing to Waste

How to Excite Kitty's Mind

Cats are thoughtful, clever, and innovative. Without stimulation they can become ill-tempered, bored, and resentful. They need things to play with, to figure out, and to think about, or they will go quietly nuts.

It doesn't take an animal rights activist to notice that cats stuck in cages at the zoo, or in those appalling traveling shows that sometimes visit shopping malls, are neurotic. Many suffer from what behaviorists call "zoochosis," which means animal neurosis. Animals in danger of losing their minds develop those back and forth, 'round and 'round movements, such as pacing and circling, and use them in the same way people chant mantras: The repetition creates a rhythm and a pattern that can help the brain escape powerful stresses and endless boredom.

Cats need, desire, and appreciate satisfying challenges. Particularly during kittenhood and adolescence, but not only then. After a day of stimulation and challenge, they can collapse in a contented heap beside you when you get home from a hard day at work.

The toy chest is not only somewhere to stow kitty's stuff, but eventually a treasure trove of old favorites to reminisce over as kitty gets all gray around the whiskers.

SIMPLE AND CHEAP THINGS YOU CAN DO

If you lived in a dirtpatch without a dime, you could scrounge up things like discarded feathers and leaves, a handful of grass (beware of pesticides), dried flowers, and empty boxes or twigs that would keep your cat occupied, as well as keep you in stitches. Here are some simple, cost-free but adored amusements.

1. Teach your cat to imitate a golden retriever: Scrunch up bits of tinfoil and roll them into balls, then toss and flick them around. Cats can be pretty adept at pouncing on, retrieving, and eventually amusing themselves for hours with these shiny silver toys. Bobbi Hoffman, a teacher, tosses paper balls down the stairs, and her cat, Kiwi, bounds down and brings them proudly back to be put in play again, just as a dog would return a thrown stick. Other people use pine cones and nut shells. The PETA office cats enjoy retrieving little dime-store plastic lizards (which, believe it or not, they recognize as lizards, often chewing off their tails and dragging them around in their mouths, looking mighty proud)!

2. Cats have been known to inhale unusual substances that make them start doing the cat equivalent of giggling

uncontrollably. Jack, one of the PETA office cats, adores shoes. Should someone slip theirs off under a desk, he can be found upside down with his head stuck in the toe part and a really silly grin on his face. Richard Vialls of Lancashire, England, meanwhile, is trying to determine what is in the ink of the *New Scientist* magazine. His cat slobbers all over his copies of it and then nuzzles into "the revolting mess," clearly getting high.

A sure bet, however, is catnip. You can buy starter catnip and grow it in the garden, a window box, or indoors under greenhouse lights. (Keep the seed packet handy for when your local police officer drops by—their leaves look a lot like marijuana.) Then stuff whole or ground-up leaves into a square of cotton gauze. Most cats will roll on their backs and purr and gaze dreamily into space with one of these mildly stimulating sachets between their paws. Wouldn't you *love* to know what they are thinking at such times?

Another good source of organic catnip is National Animal, at 7000 U.S. #1 North, St. Augustine, FL 32095 (1-800-274-7387). There's catnip spray, too. Available in a can from Four Paws (50 Wireless Boulevard, Hauppauge, NY 11788 (516-434-1100) for about $6.

If your cat has started to wear a bandanna and his meow sounds like "wow," it may be time to move up to Black Tie Mountain Lion Catnip, which is organic, handpicked, berib-

TOP TIP: Organic catnip is available from Cat Faeries, 3964 26th Street, Department BF, San Francisco, CA 94131.

boned, and boxed. It is pure buds and so potent that just one bud will do the trick. Write Mountain Lion, P.O. Box 120, Forest Hill, WV 24935 (304-466-1437). A small "gourmet" bud sprig in a little plastic case costs about $7.50, including shipping and handling.

Bored with catnip? The people at The Cat House (110 Crowchild Trail, NW, Calgary, Alberta T2N 4R9, Canada, 1-800-MEOW-CAT) suggest trying honeysuckle. Cats agree, behaving ludicrously in its presence: drooling over it, rolling on it, smiling like dolphins at it, just as they would with the "C weed."

3. Create a "bag of tricks" by placing an empty paper grocery bag on the floor. When kitty enters the bag, which is inevitable, sneak up and move your fingers lightly along the side. Using several bags will provide rapid-fire hiding places during finger attacks. If you are otherwise engaged, your ever-imaginative cat will still find the bag amusing sans fingers. (Empty cardboard boxes are deeply appreciated, too.)

There is even a washable, cotton/polyethylene sack you can buy that makes the sort of sound a constantly rustled paper bag would. See page 35 for ordering information for the Kitty Krinkle Sack.

4. Recycle the pull tab from juice containers—into a cat toy. Don't ask me why, but most cats will play with these little doodads until they keel over from exhaustion.

5. In the evenings, try dousing the lights and run the beam from a pencil flashlight or a very low-wattage laser pointer over the carpet and up the wall. As with all games, do let the cat win sometimes.

6. Here's something useful to do with the odd sock you

pull out of the dryer. When you've given up searching for its mate, shove some catnip into the toe section, add some cotton ball or any sort of safe stuffing, and then tie this newly-made ball off by knotting the top of the sock. A piece of string tied to that will allow you to drag the old sock enticingly about the floor, or it's just as wonderful given to your cat as is.

7. Possibly the *only* ethical use of a fishing pole (although a long stick works just as well): "Cast" a piece of string out toward your cat, having secured a bit of fluff, plastic bait worm, or other squiggly bit to the end, and reel or pull it back in.

8. Finally, walking on the beach or in the park? Don't forget to pick up feathers, seaweed, and other interesting but harmless discards that your cat(s) will find smelly and fascinating to play with. (I dry seaweed first and then tie it to a doorknob or to a string and drag or dangle it about). A few feathers tied together make for a super game of pounce on the prey.

OFF THE SHELF

Now, a few toys I'd recommend dipping into the, er, kitty for:

THE CAT DANCER

Amazingly simple, yet absolutely tantalizing, the Cat Dancer is a twizzly bit of fluff on the end of a flexible wire that you twirl around. Some people cheat and tie it to a doorknob, which can work well, but cats far prefer having you attached to one end of it. Write Cat Dancer Products, Inc., 2448 Industrial Drive, Neenah, WI 54956.

THE INCREDIBLE CAT TUNNEL

The PETA office cats go rabid for this bizarre little object, which they use as an instant amusement park the moment we throw it onto a floor. It weighs nothing and collapses to less than nothing, so you can toss it in a drawer; but it unfolds into a flexible, see-through net tunnel that can be curved around corners or laid out straight.

It truly *does* convert "any indoor space into a fun play area" as advertised and is worth shelling out the approximately $50 for a ten-foot version. (The five-footer is about $28, also excellent.) It is available from Data Find, P.O. Box 665, Aiea, HI 96701-0665, (808-488-8911).

THE KITTY KRINKLE SACK

Unlike the Cat Tunnel, this solid sack allows cats to hide without being seen. It is available from Flexi-Mat at 2244 South Western Avenue, Chicago, IL 60608 (773-376-5500) for about $16. Their logo is "End Cat Boredom!" This machine-washable, durable, crawl-in bag satisfies cat curiosity and lets two cats play hide-and-seek together.

THE CAT TRACK

This is a fabulous, fascinating, and thoroughly annoying Ping-Pong ball in a plastic container. It can be ordered from Drs. Foster and Smith, P.O. Box 100, Rhinelander, WI 54501 (800-562-7169) and costs $8.99.

COSMIC CATNIP SCRATCHING POST

Whoever marketed this is a genius: It is basically a brick of corrugated cardboard with a bit of catnip rubbed on it. However, as soon as claws meet paper, even the most sedate cats seem to "dig." Write Cosmic Pet Products, 133 South Burnhams Boulevard, Hagerstown, MD 21740 (301-797-3115).

CAT TV

These videos of flitting fish, birds singing their hearts out, and all manner of interesting animals putting on *The Gong Show* for cats meet mixed reactions from feline audiences. Some cats can't get enough and almost meld themselves to the screen, fascinated; others yawn and nod off the way people do when faced with the umpteenth rerun of *Gilligan's Island*. Here are a couple to try (videos are available at many pet supply shops or directly from distributors):

1. *Video Catnip*, $20 from PetAvision, Inc. (1-800-521-7898).

2. *Betty Bird*, Approximately $19.95 from Feline Features, 7040 West Palmetto Park Road, Department 2105, Boca Raton, FL 33433.

THE KRAZY BALL

If your arm gets tired, consider a motorized (!) ball. The Krazy Ball takes an AA battery and the effort out of your play. It is available from Drs. Foster and Smith at 800-562-7169 for about $14, including shipping and handling. (This company has other neat toys, such as a sisal hanging scratching post, complete with bell and rattle, so it's worth calling just for a catalog.)

MOUSE CHASE

Mouse Chase is a ball of fluff on the end of a string, atop a plush scratching post. The motor inside makes the mouse jump and swivel and move about erratically. This toy is received in much the same way most little boys receive an electric train set: You cannot pull them away from it for the first few weeks, then they forget all about it. Nevertheless, if you have about $45 you don't need, your cat will appreciate its charms.

> TIP: While some toys are kitty self-contained, both species will miss out on maximum fun if you avoid those that demand your involvement.

4

Healthy of Tooth

FIRST, THE FANGS

According to R. Yelland, a veterinarian affiliated with The American Veterinary Dental College, "Eighty percent of cats over four years old have periodontic disease." How has this happened?

Traditionally, kitties have kept their mouths fresh and teeth clean by chewing fresh, raw grasses and gnawing on the bones of rodents who couldn't sprint well. Today, it's mostly mushy food (even dry kibble turns to mush in the mouth), so gums are vulnerable to infection (first sign: bad breath, but periodontal disease can lead to serious systemic infections) and teeth to decay. The modern cat's teeth (thirty per cat) sometimes shred! Not a pretty sight and sometimes painful for puss, to boot.

I once knew a parrot who had been kept in a cage in a dental hygienist's office. This poor bird had endured a miserable life, not only deprived of other birds to preen and talk to, but forced to endure a steady diet of piped-in showtunes! For four years she watched, all day, every day, as a person in a white smock plopped people into a chair and cleaned their teeth. When she was finally rescued from her life as a living ornament, this smart bird couldn't wait to try her "hand" at dentistry. When the aviary door was open, she would fly over to the nearest human being, hop onto their shoulders, and pry open their mouths, all the better to insert her beak into those hard-to-reach nooks and crannies! As disconcerting as this could be for unsuspecting visitors, they had to admit she did a fine job!

The parrot doesn't make house calls, so here are three easy things you can do:

1. If your cat is still a kitten, start his tooth-care regimen in the privacy and comfort of your own home. Gently rub your finger along kitty's gums and teeth. Use a little garlicky water if you like (crush one or one-half clove of garlic into one-fourth cup of lukewarm water). Do this as often as it is tolerated, once a week or several times a day.

As the little nipper grows, you may wish to pick up a bumpy, plastic fingerguard from your veterinarian, or sneakily substitute an extra-soft toothbrush while practicing your very best cooing, bedside manner. The important thing is to stimulate the gums and rub away the grime and slime. You can use toothpaste, but not so much, you won't want to leave any residue in kitty's mouth. Some people believe plantain leaves make a good cat mouthwash. Here's the rinse recipe: Steep one tablespoon of leaves in one-half cup of boiling hot water for five minutes. Strain, cool down, and use as a mouthwash. Use twice a day for ten to fourteen days. Alternatively, use the herb in the morning and apply vitamin E (fresh out of the capsule) to the gums with your fingers at night. (This treatment is very soothing.)

Many cats are finicky about most types of toothpaste and absolutely *loathe* mint flavoring. In fact, some cats will bite their human companion's lips if they smell the stuff. There are exceptions, of course. Loretta Hirsh, former president of the Washington Humane Society, had a ginger and white "baker's cat," Jasper, who *adored* mint and liked his chin rubbed. No fool, Jasper found how to enjoy both pleasures simultaneously by standing on the bathroom sink and rubbing his chin over the toothbrushes in the wall holder. (The Hirshes report that Jasper also loved to roll olives along the floor using his chin!)

2. Have your cat's teeth examined by a veterinarian at least once a year. Should your cat have to undergo any procedure for which anaesthesia is required, seize the opportunity to have his teeth professionally cleaned!

3. Petrodex Dental Care Kit costs about $8 and is available from St. Jon Pet Care, 1656 West 240th Street, Harbor City, CA 90710 (310-326-2720).

> TOP TIP: If you notice your cat's gums are bleeding, or if your cat starts to chew slowly or eat out of only one side of his mouth, something is undoubtedly amiss and requires your attention.

5

Claws

NOW, THE FEET

Cat scratch fever doesn't have to mean a choice between shredded couches or "off with their claws!" Cats *have* to scratch. We may not know all the reasons, but among them are the need to mark territory, nail conditioning, play, and exercise. Even proper stretching requires scratching. So, while it's important not to prevent cats from scratching, you can control the where, if not the why.

Declawing is like taking a hatchet to a hangnail. It is illegal in England, not because the land of my birth is a nation of eccentrics, but because the operation is decidedly cruel. In fact, the British Veterinary Association calls declawing "an unnecessary mutilation." In North America, both the Humane Society of the United States and the American Humane Association frown on the procedure.

Contrary to most people's idea, surgery involves severing

not just nails, but whole phalanges (up to the first joint), including bone, ligaments, and tendons! Possible complications of this surgery include pain, damage to the radial nerve, hemorrhage, bone chips that prevent healing, and recurrent infections.

In the United States, the Association of Veterinarians for Animal Rights (AVAR) has appealed to fellow practitioners to refuse to perform such surgeries. According to AVAR president, Dr. Nedim Buyukmihci, "Declawing is unacceptable because the suffering and disfigurement it causes is not offset by any benefits to the cat. Correcting deficiencies in the cat's environment is the appropriate course of action. . . ."

Dr. Nichols H. Dodman of Tuft's University School of Veterinary Medicine adds, "I find the declawing of cats abhorrent and inhumane." Dr. Louis J. Camuti, a practicing vet for more than forty years, puts it this way: "I wouldn't declaw a cat if you paid me $1,000 a nail!" 'Nuf said!

One *Cat Fancy* magazine reader wrote, "Can you please tell me why my five-year-old Persian no longer runs and plays since being declawed? It's been eight weeks since surgery. Before being declawed she was full of life; she played ball and ran and jumped with me every day. Now all she does is sleep and eat. It's very sad to see a cat who was once so full of life now so lifeless. Do you have any idea why she is like this now?"

How I wish the writer could turn back the clock. What she is seeing is that the scars from declawing are not just physical, but psychological as well, because "doing their nails" is as normal for cats as the need to stretch. If their natural instinct to manicure is thwarted, they can go a bit cuckoo.

Some cats get so shell-shocked by declawing that their personalities change, and they simply refuse to use the litterbox again, proving that there's more than one way to ruin furniture coverings! One theory is that when they use the box after surgery, their feet are so tender they associate their new pain with the box, permanently. Another is that because they can no longer mark with their claws, they mark with urine instead. Whatever a declawed cat is thinking, the results can be unpleasant. Other declawed kitties become so traumatized by this ugly, painful, and unethical surgery that they end up spending their maladjusted lives perched on top of doors and refrigerators, out of reach of real and imaginary predators against whom they no longer have any adequate defense. They not only lose their grip, but their grip on reality, seeming unable to concentrate on much beyond the loss of their nether bits, their vulnerability, and their feelings of betrayal.

Chris Lewis, who lives in Rockville, Maryland, almost lost his declawed cat, Phanoah, when the cat lost his footing while walking along a balcony rail and fell eleven stories to the pavement below. It is true that an innovative veterinarian once outfitted an injured police dog with a stunning new set of glass teeth, but sadly no cat who has lost her mittens has had a replacement lot sewn back on. Chris now keeps the balcony door firmly locked.

Declawing involves removal of parts of cats' toes. This is a problem because cats actually walk *on their toes* rather than on the balls of their feet as we do. If you watch a declawed cat, you will see that some of them move like slightly inebriated drivers trying desperately to walk that chalk line for the nice trooper who has pulled them over for "weaving." That is because they have a hard time balancing properly on their stumps. Gone forever is that wonderful, assured, catwalk gait the supermodels mimic at the haute couture shows in Paris.

It may be easy to see the difference in how a declawed kitty moves, but what we *can't* see is worse: The nails can actually grow back *inside* the cat's paw, causing pain but remaining invisible to the eye. Declawed cats need regular X rays to monitor this problem. Whether or not the nails grow back, declawed cats can suffer chronic back and joint pain as shoulder, leg, and back muscles weaken. No wonder cats suffering in this way may bite when scratched or stroked too hard.

Is there a solution? But, of course!

Unless she spends most days playing in the road on the hard pavement (which one sincerely hopes is not the case), kitty's claws will have sharp hooks on them. To prevent furniture damage, that hook simply needs to be snipped off or blunted.

You can get kitty to do the job herself or you can lend a hand.

SIMPLE AND FREE

1. Get thee to the nearest patch of woods, beach, or gardening store; linger a while and enjoy yourself, then bring home a nice stump. Naturally, foragers can't be choosers, but if you can get your mitts on a chunk of tree that's about eighteen inches in diameter and three to four feet tall, kitty will be able to stretch her claws up on it nicely and then sit atop it afterward.

If the world's perfect stump is not in evidence, settle for

anything: Any stump is better than no stump at all. To get the bugs out of it, leave it outside, exposed to the sun and off the ground. After about a week, bump it around a little bit outside to dislodge persistent insect squatters and drag it indoors, preferably placing it on an easy-to-vacuum surface or newspaper.

Your mini-tree is now ready for kitty to dull her nails and pull off old growth ("sharpen" is a misnomer), exactly as nature intended.

2. In the same way sharks can detect a drop of blood in a mile of ocean, cats' sensitive noses pick up even very faint odors. So, smear a drop of cologne or flea dip on any material kitty is fond of tearing up, and she will probably veer away from it like a jet fighter at an air show.

3. You can also deter cats by covering off-limits furniture temporarily with something slippery, such as contact paper. If left on for a while, cats will move on to something else (hopefully, something you don't mind them scratching) and forget that that was their favorite spot. It's a good idea to put a scratching post near where they normally scratch (at least for a while if it is an inconvenient location), and, like the soldiers at Dunsinane sneaking up on Macbeth, keep moving it gradually to a more convenient spot.

A note to parents of infants and young children: Don't worry needlessly about your cat seriously scratching a child. Cats are generally careful around children, recognizing them as vulnerable, part of the family, and potentially naive, and sheath their claws even during play. All should be well unless you put the cat in a position where she must fight for

TIP: You may need to assist young, naïve, or habituated cats by politely disentangling their claws when they start scratching on something precious, carrying them to the post, and helping them get started by making scratching gestures on the wood with their paws. If you react to a mistake with harsh words, screams, or hasty, threatening body movements, this could backfire, hopelessly souring kitty to your suggestions.

her life against an unsupervised and unruly child strong enough to try to squash the breath out of her torso. Mothers can worry about all sorts of things, but freak accidents aside, cat scratches aren't among them.

SIMPLE AND CHEAP

Cats love shredding old phone books (new ones, too, actually), but if you prefer not to have your home covered in shredded paper, try these solutions:

1. Rustle up a serviceable cat scratching post by covering a wooden box with carpet remnants and anchoring it by putting sand inside at the base.

Or buy some scratching posts (three is *not* a crowd). There are also scratching boxes made of cardboard or sisal. They lie flat on the floor and are cheap enough to scatter

> TOP TIPS: You can also help your cat get interested in a post by sprinkling it with catnip, hanging toys from it and playing with your cats on and around it. Keep him or her interested by sprinkling new catnip on it weekly. (We have Saturday "catnip parties" at my house—*sooo* cute! Fun for the whole family!)

about. One favorite is the Cosmic Catnip Post. Don't forget to leave a post or scratching box near your kitty's favorite nighttime sleeping place. Cats love to scratch their nails when they wake up.

In the Johnson household, four-year-olds Jasmine and Ariel have persuaded their people to staple carpet samples (about two feet by three feet) onto the wall near door jambs starting at about six inches off the floor. This allows a good stretch and scratch while keeping an eye on two rooms at once.

Vertical posts should also be sturdy and tall enough for a cat to stretch out fully (a wobbly post will frighten a cat away). It should also be covered in a *rough*-textured carpet turned inside out, or sisal. Cardboard posts need to be changed when worn out, or your cat will become frustrated and lose interest.

2. Invest in a decent pair of nail clippers (available from your veterinarian and from pet supply catalogs and stores). Be sure they are kept sharp.

Cats' claws must be *carefully* trimmed. Press the paw between your fingers and thumb (as shown in the diagram below) to unsheathe the claws. Trim just enough to blunt them (one-eighth of an inch from the tip) but not enough to cut the quick, which can sometimes be seen outlined within the nail, ending between the tip and the bend. Only do kitty's *front* paws. Hind paws pose no threat, except during cat ninja kicking contests, and will help kitty climb trees to safety if she accidentally slips out the door. Weekly trims are recommended.

Have your veterinarian give you a "how to" demonstration the first time if you feel a bit shaky. Here are the three steps to follow:

1. Press to fully extend the nail
2. Calculate where to cut to avoid the quick
3. Trim firmly and decisively. (He who dithers about makes trimming more traumatic, plus nails may snap unless the cut is strong and firm).

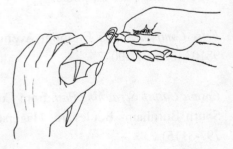

Nail Clipping

TIP: Unless major surgery is required, never leave kitty at the vet's office, no matter how nice everyone is. The people probably are nice, but your cat depends on you to guard her against evil goings-on. Every humane officer has horror stories about "what went on in the back" of even respectable-seeming clinics, e.g., crates stacked to the ceiling during a rush, animals forgotten after surgery, even fire. If you saw George C. Scott in *Hospital* you have some idea.

EASY

Take your cat to the veterinarian for regular claw trims.

Even in the best of veterinary hospitals, the scents and noises, as well as the understandable fear of the unknown, make even really sophisticated, worldly wise cats worried and scared. It is worth messing up your own life a bit to stay at your cat's side during the procedure, thus minimizing the trauma of an attack by strangers wielding metal objects. Then, whisk kitty straight home, apologize profusely, and lay on a really nice treat, or six. All may be forgiven.

Scratching post suppliers:

Felix Company, 3623 Fremont Avenue, North, Seattle, WA 98103 (206-547-0042)

Cosmic Catnip Scratching Post, from Cosmic Pet Products, 133 South Burnhams Boulevard, Hagerstown, MD 21740 (301-797-3115)

HappyCo, P.O. Box 514, Newport, RI 02840 (401-849-6337). This is an excellent catnip scratching pad that sits flat on the floor.

Soft Paws are nail caps for cats, soft vinyl caps that keep cats' nails blunt and harmless four to five times longer than routine nail trimming. The durable caps are held in place by an adhesive and are available in sizes to fit kittens and adult cats. The nail caps usually last four to six weeks, depending on the rate of nail growth and the activity level of your cat. They are easy to apply and safe for your cat. Ask your veterinarian for more information, or for a similar product called Soft Claws call Drs. Foster and Smith at 1-800-826-7206.

6

There's No Time to Kiss You When I Have Bugs in My Belly and Fleas in My Fur

Emergencies, like finding that your cat has cleverly managed to wedge her bottom inside a firewall, are not the only health and well-being concerns that demand our prompt attention. Case in point: the matter of internal and external parasites. These little devils do not visit cats in the benign way pilot fish perch on sharks' heads or little birds enter hippopotamuses' mouths to pick their teeth clean. Symbiosis is not up their alley. Worms and fleas simply besiege cats and make their lives miserable. Luckily, dealing with them will not break the piggy bank, and they are no big deal to tackle; but tackled they must be.

MORE THAN A PAIN IN THE NECK

To look at it one way, the universe is a complex system of interdependency in which one organism clings to its fragile existence through its interaction with another organism. To look at it in a slightly different way, some people spend their lives mooching off others. To a parasite, no slight intended, a cat represents a cozy, warm place to live and a twenty-four-hour-a-day, open buffet. External parasites, such as fleas, invite their friends, such as tapeworms, to move into the part of the house they're not using, i.e., your cat's intestines. In fact, they actually pack for them: Fleas eat tapeworm eggs and deposit them in their own feces, which kitty then ingests when she cleans her coat.

If enough parasites call kitty "home," they can cause severe problems, such as anemia, especially in tiny kittens and elderly cats; but even a small squatter's camp means blood and food are being taken away from your cat, and such conditions as dry skin and irritation from flea bites are offered in their place. As soon as you see even one, serve an eviction notice.

TAKE MY WORMS, PLEASE

If you live in the South, the best advice when it comes to tropical storms or external parasites is to sell up and move. However, internal parasites flunked geography, so you can't escape them even if you hightail it to the snowy peaks of Colorado. In fact, *Giardia*, a protozoan parasite, thrives in some of the prettiest rivers there.

Luckily, you can usually deal with most internal parasites all in one go, whether they are hookworms, roundworms, or tapeworms. Then there is the aforementioned bug, *Giardia*, which can be detected using a special test. Coccidia, another nonworm, is often hard to detect at all.

Cats can pick up parasites from a mud puddle, the soil,

another cat, or infected meat or greens. Hookworm larvae are particularly insidious. It can simply burrow quietly through normal skin when you are not looking.

Many worms are invisible to the naked eye, and others are so small that even people under forty who have never experienced the humiliation of squinting at a canned goods label can't see them without a magnifying glass. Others, like tapeworms, are impressively long, but are tucked away secretly where you can't find them, although tiny segments of their bodies break off and can be seen, wiggling momentarily in your cat's stool or dried into a tiny white flake, stuck on her rump, pretending to be a grain of rice. Roundworms, which are very common in kittens and often give a bloated beach ball look to a small cat's stomach, *are* visible if passed in feces. They resemble strands of Silly String.

Outside the body, all worms and worm segments die quickly, but worm eggs are very resilient and can lie in wait in grass and soil for a long, long time, until that special moment when the possibility of reinfestation becomes a reality for them.

If you see any of the symptoms of parasitism, such as diarrhea, blood or mucus in the stool, bloating, a stomach sensitive to the touch, pale gums, a dry hair coat, or malnutrition, you'll no doubt act immediately. But, just to be sure, no matter how shiny-coated and energetic your cat may be, take a sample of his stool to your veterinarian. The sample should be recent, say within twelve hours, unless you have refrigerated it.

The vet will examine the sample under the microscope and let you know what desperate little life-forms have taken up squatter's rights inside your cat. It is always possible that you'll be told your cat is worm-free when, in fact, he isn't. That means adult worms weren't in the mood to make eggs the day you collected the sample. Since evidence of tapeworms is a hit-and-miss proposition, your vet will gladly accept your suggestion that you want to worm your cat anyway.

Perhaps most important, mark your calendar in big letters and do not miss the reworming date. The first worming kills the mommy and daddy worms, but larvae must be killed after they have hatched and before they are ready to bear their own young. That makes the second worming crucial.

SHUTTING DOWN THE FLEA CIRCUS

Summer, especially in Southern states, can be very depressing for nonfleas. Flea conventions flock to enjoy the warm weather and have no compunction about partying it up for months, making your cat scratch so much he looks as if he has Saint Vitus' dance. Not that fleas don't pose problems year-round. They do.

Controlling them requires a multipronged approach.

Anticipating your less-than-welcoming response to their presence, fleas will have taken precautions to secure their territory, cleverly invading not only your cat, but your carpet and gaps or cracks in the floorboard or tile where they can lay the eggs of future flea armies. All their hiding places must be treated at the same time as you de-flea your cat.

Attack the infestation in three ways: your home (now their home, too), all bedding, and your cat.

Your Home

Spring cleaning may have been invented to thwart fleas. Vacuum the rugs; clean between cracks in tiles, floorboards, and any crevices daily during spring and summer months. Once you start looking for flea hideouts in your home, you will probably find so many gaps in the construction that you will no longer be amazed at your winter heating bills. Do not let the filled vacuum bag sit around, even for a moment. Take it and its cargo of fleas and flea eggs quickly outside and put it in the trash, otherwise fleas will walk back out the way they went in, and their eggs will hatch in the nice warm bag.

To kill larvae, you can sprinkle borax or ordinary table salt on the carpet overnight and then vacuum it up the next morning.

You can use a good flea shampoo in a mop bucket, or commercial rug cleaner, to kill whatever bits and pieces of animal life you leave behind after the vacuuming. Try to rinse afterward because these products are strong and strong smelling. They can be unpleasant, even toxic, to a cat or kitten.

Tuck cedar blocks and/or herbal sachets between the cushions of upholstered furniture.

If you choose to "bomb" your house with a commercial preparation, read the warning below about poisoning, and please be sure to keep your cat(s) away for twice the amount of time listed on the label, for added safety, and to meticulously clean/rinse away chemical residue.

Federal authorities decide what goes on these labels and are too often beholden to the industries they supposedly regulate, and they are not known for their accuracy in counseling citizenry on the use of hazardous substances. Think how cheaply you can buy a home in Love Canal; remember their assurances that Agent Orange–like insecticides could be sprayed from aircraft or sprinkled on breakfast cereal; remember how they laughed off exposure to DDT and joyously lined our children's school ceilings with asbestos.

THE OUTDOOR BREEDING GROUND

If your cat goes out onto your lawn, you might use an organic flea control product there, too. Some contain nematodes (microorganisms that eat flea larvae) and can be sprayed or sprinkled on grass and soil. These are safe for animals, birds, and humans, as well as "friendly" garden dwellers such as earthworms and ladybugs. Brand names such as Bio Flea, Halt!, Biosys, and Interrupt! can be found in pet stores and in the lawn and garden sections of hardware stores and supermarkets.

Another option is to buy some diatomaceous earth (a powder composed of the fossilized remains of one-celled algae) from the garden or swimming pool supply store and sprinkle it on your lawn. It is safe (and politically correct) to get it on your hands, but not to inhale it. Use a protective mask so as to avoid inhaling the dust and get animals out of the area during application.

THE BEDDING

Put all the cat's bedding (which includes window seat covers and your own blankets) into the washer and wash it on the *hottest* water setting with a flea shampoo *that advertises that it kills the eggs*. If in doubt, wash everything twice.

If fleas reappear, launder bedding once a week.

THE CAT

And now for the centerpiece of all this activity, the cat.

You can go the natural route, which is less toxic and usually far safer for your cat (although even these have been known to cause nasty reactions), or you can bring in the heavy toxic artillery, take your chances (and your cat's), and "nuke" the fleas.

Whichever way you go, try not to leave your cat at the vet for a flea dip or bath. Do it yourself, with help from a cat-conscious assistant if you can get one. That way, you will not have to worry that your cat has suffered a reaction that has gone unnoticed at the vet or has been left too long in a cage dryer by a busy attendant. Buying the dip or shampoo yourself means you can read the label carefully (please do) and choose the product you think is best. By the way, never bathe your cat if you don't *have* to, but if you *must* (for example, if he gets covered in soot after an ambitious run up the chimney or jumps into a bowl of barbeque sauce), always use a nonslip rubber mat in the sink or tub. Being set upon with water is one indignity; not being able to keep your footing is another. Take a hint from Heloise, who advises that, in the absence of a rubber mat, you can place a small window screen on a couple of towels at the bottom of the tub, allowing your cat to hang on while being bathed. Also, run the water before introducing cat to tub. Unless your cat is an Asiatic fishing cat, which is just what it sounds like, chances are he is scared to death of that gushing noise.

Educator Danielle Moore once lived with a cat, Bean, who would sit on the kitchen counter while she washed the dishes. Bean would reach over and place her paw in the stream coming from the faucet. Sometimes she would climb right into the sink and allow a slow flow of water to fall over her head! She was fascinated with water and would perch on the edge of the tub while Danielle bathed. Not that Bean jumps into the tub, she doesn't.

Bean was found under the hood of a truck. Before driving home one evening, the driver had thought she heard a cat meowing. She searched all around but Bean didn't call out again, so she figured the cat had run off. She drove nearly thirty miles, on the expressway and city streets, before arriving at her suburban home. Later that night, her son walked by the truck and heard the cat. Opening the hood, he found Bean perched precariously near the motor. When he lifted her out she was trembling, but she immediately began to purr in his arms.

The next day she went to live with Danielle, still covered in grit and grime. That's when Danielle learned to bathe a cat the easy way, using a towel swaddling. Here it is:

Gently wrap the cat in a towel, in the manner that a baby might be swaddled, with the feet secured and the head uncovered. A very good idea is to sew two towels together with one side left open to form a bag. Cats usually don't mind being swaddled as long as it is done gently. Don't wrap too tightly; just enough so that the cat doesn't have the ability to flail about and slide in the wet basin.

The temperature should be pleasantly warm, not hot, so that the placement into the water is almost imperceptible to the cat. Put just a few inches of water in the basin. Fill a couple of large pitchers with warm water for rinsing. Cats never liked being sprayed so don't even think about trying to turn on the faucet to rinse them off. This should all be done as quietly as possible.

With the cat's head uncovered, place him in the sink. Allow him to "get his feet wet," and speak to him in a soft and reassuring voice. With your hand or a sponge, get the towel surrounding the cat wet. Don't splash. Work a gentle baby shampoo through the fabric. Don't get the cat's head wet. You can use a sponge or washcloth on his head later. Don't work up the sort of lather you might when washing yourself. You don't want to take too long rinsing. The towel can be used to massage the lather all over the cat.

To rinse, pour the pitcher of warm water—slowly—over and under the towel. As more of the lather is rinsed away, gradually push the towel down and away from the cat. When he's all rinsed, gather him up right away in a fluffy dry towel and pat him dry. He'll want to get away from you to groom himself, so make sure he has a warm place to sit and dry off.

There are mesh bags that you can use to slip your cat into to allow you to control him during the bath. The bags can also be used to help restrain a cat for medication or manicuring. Available from Vital Visions, P.O. Box 566005, Atlanta, GA 30056, for about $24 postage paid.

A Toxic Shocker

The active ingredient in most commercial flea products is a form of nerve gas called Sevin! In fact, one company advertises its product as a "powerful chemical warfare agent used in the Persian Gulf War." I doubt many soldiers would vote to use it. Every summer, the Illinois Poison Control Center, a national authority on toxins, receives thousands of calls reporting flea pesticide poisonings of cats and dogs.

When you read most pesticide labels you will find a warning not to get it on your skin, to wash your hands after applying it, and to keep it away from children. But the label goes on to give directions that usually include rubbing the substance into the animal's coat—as if his skin would not absorb chemical poisons, too!

At People for the Ethical Treatment of Animals (PETA) we obtained a video of a tiny calico kitten in a laboratory cage, crying and experiencing racking convulsions in a flea shampoo test for a well-known manufacturer. Believe it or not, just because the kitten suffered doesn't mean the company decided not to market the product! As with many industries, the litmus test of whether or not to sell something is sometimes whether or not the company can outsell the amount of money it has to pay out in damages when consumers bring lawsuits!

One example of a potentially toxic product that was tested on animals yet appeared on store shelves is Blockade. In 1987, Hartz Mountain acknowledged that 366 animal deaths and 2,700 known animal injuries, as well as 56 human injuries, had been blamed on Blockade. Hartz pulled it from the market, tested it on cats and kittens, and then reintroduced it with the *same ingredients*! The company eventually paid the Environmental Protection Agency $45,000 to settle charges that it failed to report animal illnesses and deaths from Blockade—fat lot of good that did the animals harmed.

Using too much of a product, using it too often, or using more than one product (such as a collar, dip, and powder) can cause a dangerous or fatal overdose. Long-term effects of flea pesticides include cancer, allergies, nerve damage, and other medical problems.

So, if you decide to use chemical warfare, be very cautious. Please, never hop off to work leaving your cat alone after a dip or shampoo. If you see drooling, foaming at the mouth, body twitching, lethargy, diarrhea, difficulty breathing, difficulty moving, vomiting, or hear crying, take your cat immediately to the veterinarian *with the product you used.*

Should you choose a chemical flea collar, be sure to hang it up somewhere for a few days before getting it anywhere near your cat. Then check for any allergic reaction, such as a rash around her neck.

Young cats and elderly cats are extra-susceptible to toxic reactions, but some healthy, adult cats can suffer from them, too.

THE LOW TOXICITY ROUTE

It surprises most people to know what every pesticide company tries to keep a secret: Pesticides are unnecessary, because ordinary soap and water kill fleas! Soap penetrates the outer coating around the flea and destroys its natural defenses.

One nontoxic rinse that both kills fleas and soothes irritated skin can be made with a fresh lemon and hot water. Just slice the lemon thinly (including the peel), pour a pint of near-boiling water over it, and allow it to steep overnight. The next day, sponge the solution onto the animal's skin and let it dry or pour it into an empty spray bottle and use it as a spray (storing extra liquid in the refrigerator, but not for long).

Bear in mind that citrus scents are offensive to some cats (they are sometimes used to keep cats off furniture), so test your cat's tolerance before using them.

Gentle herbal shampoos can be quite effective and can be used as often as once a week, although too-frequent bathing can dry out your cat's skin. When shampooing, use warm water and begin with a ring of lather around the cat's neck so fleas cannot climb onto the cat's face.

Take the Darth Vader approach to flea control with the "Flea Zapper." This battery-operated comb stuns and immobilizes fleas, using an extremely low electrical charge that most animals don't seem to mind or even feel. Conked-out fleas can be combed out of the hair and tidily sealed into one of the little baggies that comes with the comb. It costs about $50 from the Kensington Marketing Group, 914-235-9300.

Homeopathic practitioners also have interesting advice on how to deal with common problems such as fleas. Dr. Edgar Sheaffer, who writes for *The Health Care Letter*, recommends combining a dietary approach, citrus dips, and remedies such as *arsenicum album, lachesis, lycopodium*, or *ledum palustre* to deal with fleas. Another homeopathic veterinarian, Dr. George Macleod, believes a regular course of homeopathic sulfur, repeated after two-week intervals, may help make a cat less prone to flea infestations. These remedies will eliminate the fleas or reduce the cat's allergic reaction to them.

A cat should look like a little person in a luxurious fur coat, not a tiny 'gator. If your cat's skin is flaky and dry, it can be more attractive to fleas than healthy skin (fleas do not win *Better Homes and Gardens* awards for how they like to live). Try adding fresh, raw foods such as sliced carrots and broccoli to your cat's food and slip a little evening primrose oil or flaxseed oil in as well.

If you do want to use a pesticide, two of the least toxic natural pesticides are pyrethrins, derived from chrysanthemum flowers, and D-limonene, an extract from orange peels. Look for formulations that contain these active ingredients.

Many animal guardians add nutritional yeast (*not* brewer's yeast) to their cat's food: The theory is that the yeast gives the blood a slightly bitter odor that a tiny flea nose can detect and reject before actually taking a bite. Fresh garlic, crushed or ground, can act as a flea repellent, too, which is why there are no Italian flea circuses.

FLEA BIRTH CONTROL

Insect growth regulators (IGRs) offer an alternative to pesticides. Sold under brand names such as Ovitrol, Fleatrol, and Precor, IGRs contain insect hormones that disrupt the life cycle of the flea by preventing eggs and larvae from developing. They can be sprayed or used in room foggers and are available from some exterminators, as well as from pet supply stores and catalogs.

There is a company called FleaBusters (1-800-666-3532) that uses a patented nontoxic sodium borate compound that it guarantees for up to one year. Several studies have shown the treatment, which can cost up to $250, to be highly effective.

TOP TIP: If flea bites and scratching at flea bites has your cat's skin raw and inflamed, Avon's Skin-So-Soft could help. Mix one and a half ounces of Skin-So-Soft to a gallon of water and use it as a shampoo. It has soothing properties that most cat people swear by. Aloe Vera can also be used to quiet down hot, itchy skin and is harmless if licked off.

7

Two Cats Are Better Than One

Who says so? Well, for starters, the cats sitting on death row at your local pound or shelter. Even for the snobs among them, sharing a home with another cat seems an infinitely more enjoyable proposition than that one-way trip to the back room. Not that I'm advocating cramming your house full of cats. I'm not. Things can go very wrong when a cat guardian becomes a cat "collector" and ends up overdoing it. But two cats make perfect sense, for you and for them.

If you love having one cat snuggled up to you, you'll adore having two. There are more subtle advantages as well. Anyone who has shared a bed with a cat knows that cats subscribe to the theory that too much uninterrupted sleep is bad for your health. When you have two cats and one stands on your windpipe in the middle of the night, demanding that you get up to play "where's the mouse?" they'll have each other. You can escort them both into the living room, close the door, and go back to bed.

Never fear that, were you to open your door and let one other cat walk through it, the current Ms. or Mr. Kitty wouldn't lavish as much attention on you. That's just nonsense—and a nasty, selfish thought.

While two cats cannot live as cheaply as one (ask yourself, do your kids really need to go to college?), they do deliver twice as much affection. It makes sense. The more satisfied and happy your cat is, the less cranky and neurotic she will be.

Cats are social beings, and as much as they love you, they are only "whole" when there's another cat around. Imagine if you lived with a gorilla. No matter how nice she was, you'd still want to talk to another human being once in a while. Ever see one lion, living alone in the jungle? No, there's always a group of lions (okay, a pride), lollygagging around, their arms wrapped around each other, cleaning bits of congealed impala off each other's faces.

Truly well-adjusted cats seem to float along, inches off the carpet, exuding good vibrations, stopping only to rub up against your legs and purr down your neck. If you've got two of them doing this, the only thing you'll miss is earplugs.

The main worry you may have is that your cat-in-residence will have an instant hissy-fit when the newcomer comes through the door. This is quite probable. Male cats have a reputation for being slightly more likely to fire up the Welcome Wagon than the womenfolk, but cats, overall, are not known for their magnanimity. However, even the most theatrical episodes of spitting jealousy fade. Remember Moomin and Jarvis, the two devoted Siamese cats I mentioned in the introduction to this book. Although at one time Jarvis would have bet the bank that he wouldn't want to share his life with Moomin, before long they were so devoted to each other that I'm sure he would have given his life for her.

Where to Get Kitty Number Two

In this day and age, pet shop purchases are not only politically incorrect but absolutely out of the question. They create a market for cats at a time when humane societies are tearing their hair out over the pet overpopulation crisis. According to recent figures on such dismal matters, more than 27 million cats and kittens every year are unceremoniously booted through the front doors of animal shelters or abandoned in the countryside to starve to death while learning to eat berries without a "how to" manual.

My recommendation is be a model citizen. Rescue a cat. Grant clemency to an innocent cat or kitten condemned to death row at your local pound or shelter. Think twice about getting a purebred or "designer cat." Many have genetic problems resulting from their manipulation at human hands. Take, for example, the Persian, bred for that pathetic Cabbage Patch Doll face that barely allows normal breathing, or the Flame Point Siamese who, as a result of inbreeding to produce artificial colors at the tips (or points) of their tails, ears, and feet, suffers from weepy eyes. In my book, mongrels are the most! Although, if you must have a Siamese or some other breed of cat, many shelters keep breed lists and work with breed rescue clubs. They are only too happy to match you up with the type of cat you fancy.

TOP TIP: If you can, take two cats or kittens from the same family—two kittens, for example, or a mother and her son. There is extra security in having been together from the start, and there will be no problems with introductions.

THE BASIC RULES

Whatever the origins of your new family member, whisk her directly to the veterinarian to have everything checked: gums (for anemia caused by hookworm), temperature (for feverish illness), red blood count (for feline leukemia), and on and on until your veterinarian can afford to buy a country estate. Oh, and make sure Kitty Number One is up to date on vaccinations.

Set aside a separate room in your home (not your bedroom, unless you want major tantrums from the ruling Ms. Puss) in which to treat the newcomer for anything that ails her and to allow a couple of days of peace and quiet to get over the stress of travel and transfer.

Use as many bowls as you have cats. You aren't reenacting the Oliver Twist story wherein all the orphans have to grub for their morsels. With multiple bowls, one avoids unseemly spats, keeps the peace, and preserves everyone's dignity.

Getting to Know Each Other

Introducing one cat to another can be stressful enough to make even Emily Post swear out loud. Sure, some first encounters do go smoothly, but most cats look upon the arrival of Kitty Number Two in the same way a young maid, waking up in the middle of the night to find teeth in her neck, views Dracula. Just remember, any minor inconvenience in the beginning pales in comparison to the dose of double love that may last two decades. It's worth it. Trust me, and follow my advice.

Give Kitty Number Two enough room to escape the wrath of Kitty Number One. Provide access for Kitty Number Two to hide, i.e., avoid staging the introduction in a small, unfurnished room. If you can observe unseen from outside, do. Second best, sit there, and ignore them. Force yourself to ignore all the carryings-on (unless Kitty Number One is doing something truly life-threatening, like shoving Kitty Number Two out of a sixth-floor window). If you can't look away, your "old" cat may put on a bigger show to try to win your apparently lost affections and to impress you with how gallantly she can defend the household from an intruder.

If things get too tense, bring out the tinfoil balls or some other toys. If you start batting something about, you may lure one of the cats into the game, allowing them to forget their apprehensions about each other, let their guard down, and perhaps have fun.

Whenever you see the opportunity, reassure Kitty Number One that she is still your absolute favorite by doing a lot of cooing and stroking and shoveling food in her direction. Remember to always keep the bowls far apart: Cats hate eating in front of strangers.

IF IT DOESN'T WORK OUT

Once in a while, two cats seem destined to despise each other unto death. If that happens, or for some other reason you know that having another cat in the house is not going to work, it is imperative to take every precaution when looking for the next home for Kitty Number Two. Too many cats end up shuffled, like bags of laundry, from one place to another. This leads to trauma and confusion and produces unhappy and neurotic cats.

Be tough. The words "I'll take that cat" do not guarantee a good home. Sad to say, it is far better to take Kitty Number Two to a well-run shelter (i.e., one that does not give animals to laboratories and has a sound adoption policy and sterilization requirements) than to pass her on to someone who thinks cats are cute, but who hasn't thought through the lifetime commitment every cat requires and deserves. That means you will have to put on your inspector's cap,

ANOTHER ICE-BREAKING TIP: Make the initial intro after a big meal, when kitties are inclined to want a good sleep more than a good fight. Patience is a virtue. Give 'em lots of time to make adjustments—sometimes it can take months for the relationship to gel.

visit the prospective home yourself, check veterinary references, and ask questions. Again, *don't settle for anything less than the best*, because your temporary friend's life and lifetime happiness depend on it.

RESOURCES

Guide to the Sale or Giveaway of a Dog or Cat. Free. Send a self-addressed stamped envelope to PETA, 501 Front Street, Norfolk, VA 23510, marked "Placement Guide."

The Washington Humane Society's Guide to the Sale or Giveaway of a Dog or Cat. Send a self-addressed stamped envelope to the Washington Humane Society, 7319 Georgia Avenue, NW, Washington, DC 20012.

8

Forget the Dating Game

Boys will be boys, but tomcats make boys look like angels. When your little "Tommy" becomes a real "Tom," which happens at about ten months of age, he will want to exert his sexual maturity—in many different ways.

When you wisely refuse to let him outside to have his ears torn to shreds by more experienced tomcats, he may have a pouty fit. In tomcats, pouty fits aren't events to look forward to. However, during such stressful times, your cat can't suppress his hormonally caused urges, so there is no point in your making a fuss. He will only resent you. Accept that he has become "a man." Here is what you can expect, and this is what you can do.

One testosterone-induced, macho posturing you can expect from an intact male cat is that he will back up to your furniture and spray urine all over it. His wild and free ancestors have marked their territory in this way since the dawn of time, their musky odor deterring invasion by other male cats anxious to settle down and start families. In most households, this does not go over too well. Always remind yourself, however, that he didn't ask to be domesticated. We brought him indoors, so we get to clean up.

Some human males have a major problem even thinking about the minor surgery that will stop Tom adding to, or wanting to add to, the feline overpopulation crisis. Just whisper the word "castration," and a ghastly pallor falls over men's faces. The words "Let's remove Tom's testicles" is apparently a direct assault on their own manhood.

During these times, it is up to a woman to show her strength. The surgery is simple, and while Tom will not retain his youthful soprano voice, he will stop caring about sex. Neutering also prevents testicular cancer. It is also worth noting that, like that famous cartoon skunk (Pepe LePew), male cats can detect the telltale scent of a female in heat miles away. Unlike Ulysses, however, they cannot plug their ears with wax and lash themselves to ships' masts to avoid the sirens' call. You will have to do the humane version of that for them, and that means neutering.

As for girl cats, at about five and a half to six months, their behavior can become so unsettling that it is easy to see that, were they human, they would be experimenting with makeup and risking ankle health in four-inch stilettos.

Part of the secret cat plan to conquer the world must be to have their females come into heat almost nonstop, and to come back into heat immediately after giving birth. No opportunity to reproduce is ever missed.

If your Ms. Kitty is in a breeding frame of mind, she may make weird noises that can only help you understand how the word "caterwaul" originated. Female Siamese cats are in a class by themselves here. In moments of acute romantic distress, they can sound like a horror movie scream queen. It is a wonder any male gets within a football field of them.

Your cat may also contort herself into bizarre shapes that look as if someone dropped a flatiron on her back, and she may snap at you, literally, if you cannot or do not produce a handsome male prince to woo her.

During these times, your cat will resent you in the deep and soulful way a human sixteen-year-old resents his parents for not letting him jump parked cars on a Harley Davidson. However, should you be tempted to let kitty out, or should you find yourself dialing a stud service, STOP: Don't touch that dial or that door!

Temporary solutions do not solve lifetime, recurring problems. Not only that, but, in Thomas's case, if you let him out, he is almost guaranteed to get ugly, painful, abscessed ears and other battle wounds, such as a scratched eye or nose, that will require expensive veterinary attention. (Not to mention feline AIDS, for which there's no vaccine or cure!)

In Thomasina's case, her youthful disposition will be snatched away by endless numbers of litters of demanding young 'uns, who will all need shots and what-not and are very hard to place in a kitten-crowded world.

Try this for an amazing fact: If one female cat has a litter every six months (which is normal), each litter consisting of four kittens, half of whom are females who survive and breed, the original mother cat will be responsible for thirty-six cats in just eighteen months. (The chart illustrates the equation.)

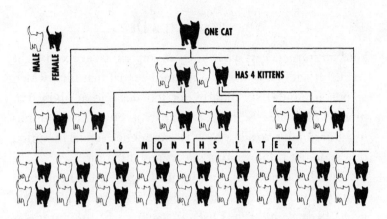

MALE FEMALE · ONE CAT · HAS 4 KITTENS · 1 6 MONTHS LATER

GETTING "FIXED"

Luckily, kitties of both genders can be made to forget the desires of the flesh. Thanks to sterilization, in the blink of an eye, or rather, the snip of a pair of surgical scissors, your cat can become sensible and settled again. Your postsurgical puss will live happily ever after and devote all his or her love to . . . you! While it is unnatural, so is eating food from a can, sleeping in a bed, and living with human beings.

There are other, not inconsequential, benefits to sterilization.

Spayed cats whose uteruses are removed during surgery cannot get uterine cancer, and studies show that spayed cats who just have their ovaries removed are less likely to get uterine cancer in their older years. Obviously, cats spayed either way cannot get cancer of the ovaries without making it into *Ripley's Believe It or Not.*

Castrated males are less inclined to prostate cancer and (as mentioned on page 71) cannot contract testicular cancer.

73

When to Do the Deed

You can sterilize cats when they are mere tots: at six to eight weeks of age. Or you can wait until sexual maturity, which comes at around six months for females and at about ten months for males. Some veterinarians prefer to wait, thinking it preferable to allow a cat to experience sexual maturity; others do not think waiting makes any difference.

Should you hold off, be careful. If your female comes in heat, you will have to wait until the first break in her heat cycle, because most vets balk at spaying when the uterus is full of blood. Should kitty have a sexual encounter, do not let that deter you from taking her to the vet as soon as she goes out of heat. Don't let your cat have "just one litter."

Get That Cat Out of There!

More and more veterinarians realize that recovery from any surgery can be hampered by stress, such as the stress of being under the control of strangers in a strange environment. Conversely, nothing makes recovery smoother than being in a quiet, secure place, tended to by someone you love and trust. Home wins out over the animal hospital.

Always insist, if necessary, on collecting your cat as soon after surgery as is safe. Avoid even one overnight stay, if you possibly can. If you work, try scheduling surgery for a Friday, so you can have the weekend with the patient. A two-day hospital stay is out of the question unless your cat needs elaborate medical care.

Should you fear a medical emergency, get a cat carrier ready and gas up the car in case you need to take the patient to an emergency hospital for attention. Comfort yourself with the knowledge that, had you left kitty at the veterinarian's office where he was neutered, there would almost certainly not have been anyone on duty there overnight to notice any problem, let alone deal with it effectively.

THE HOME RECOVERY CENTER

Set aside a very clean bed (topped with a clean, cotton sheet) in a quiet room and make sure your cat has no opportunities to pole vault herself onto tall cabinets or perform other activities that may separate the stitches. Your bedroom is probably ideal as this is the most secure, comforting room in your home. I wouldn't recommend the bathroom, even if yours is cozy and warm. Your cat wants to be with you, not alone after a stressful experience. You'll also avoid the problem that a couple in Sweden had when they put their two cats in the bathroom, and the cats turned on the shower taps and flooded the house.

Place fresh cat litter and fresh water nearby. Monitor your feline patient to make sure she doesn't disturb the stitches by overlicking, and that she starts drinking and eating enthusiastically after the anaesthetic has worn off. Linger at the bedside to murmur reassuring words about liberation from the burdens of parenthood.

Over the next two weeks, seize opportune moments, as when your cat has a leg pointed at the ceiling, to take discreet peeks to ensure that the surgical site hasn't become infected. If in doubt, call or visit the vet.

In past years, most veterinary schools taught that animals were stoic and somehow didn't feel pain as we do. The same sort of ignorant thing used to be said of infants and human slaves!

Such teaching has meant that a zillion cats have been left to suffer in silence from major surgery, such as spaying. If your vet is from "the old school," he may not realize that times have changed and that the cat's central nervous system allows your precious to feel every bit as much pain as we do. Bring him up to date or consider a new vet.

While fears of addiction used to stop doctors from prescribing medications, most vets have figured out how unlikely it is that your cat will end up robbing convenience stores to feed his or her drug habit. Insist on painkillers for your puss.

Most laypeople have enough common sense to realize that denying cats painkillers is bunk, but patients and patients' guardians still have a scary tendency to defer to authority; so it's good to listen to the vet's advice with your heart and your head. Put yourself in your cat's place, would *you* want painkillers? If the answer is yes, *demand* them.

If kitty is male, the surgery is minor. Although some swelling may give him a walk like John Wayne for a few days, he should be fit as a fiddle almost immediately after he wakes up.

If kitty is female, the surgery is major, so give complete recovery seven to ten days. After that, neither of you need ever look back (except to admire kitty's derriere).

RESOURCES

Any veterinarian with an operating room is equipped to perform spay and neuter surgeries. Prices vary tremendously.

While some vets are too mean to help with the overpopulation crisis and will moan on about people in Cadillacs driving their cat to a cheap spay, many vets are kind souls who do their community service by providing a low-cost incentive to sterilization. And some who could not care less about much more than their businesses still realize they can acquire more long-term patients via this brief encounter!

If you are truly strapped for cash, ask your local humane society or county Society for the Prevention of Cruelty to Animals (SPCA) if it operates a low-cost spay and neuter clinic or a program in cooperation with local veterinarians who reduce their fees.

Or, try calling 1-800-248-7729 for SPAY-USA, which gives referrals in over 800 locations.

9

Cats Aren't Crazy about Traveling

Barring a cataclysmic event such as a planet about to collide with your house, or your boss's announcement that you are being transferred to the Lower Ganges Basin, it is usually a very bad idea to contemplate moving your cat any greater distance than from the chair to the couch.

Nine hundred and ninety-nine cats out of a thousand, possibly more, loathe getting into a car, let alone having the car move out of the driveway, and most will hate you long after hell has frozen over if you have the audacity to buy them an airline ticket. Birds fly, not cats. (In the United States trains stopped taking cats and other animals in the 1980s for reasons not even Amtrak or the people at *Trains* magazine remember.)

However, if you tread very carefully, it is possible to manage kitty's travel plans and emerge smelling like catnip.

MUST YOU DO THIS AT ALL?

This is the million-dollar question. Obviously, if you are a sensible person who has to move, your cat is part of your family, and you will not be casting about for new "parents" for your kitty. That is only an option if you think of a cat as a replaceable, insentient object, like yard-sale bric-a-brac, and readers of this book do not think of cats in that way.

Do you have to go to wherever it is that you are thinking of going? I am quite serious. If the answer is yes and the trip is a relatively quick out-and-back one, perhaps the solution is not to pack kitty's valise, but to let her wait safely at home for your return.

"Safely at home" does not mean being holed up at the veterinarian's. Only sadists would dream of leaving a child in a cage in a hospital, exposed to diseases and the cries of others in distress, and the same goes for kitty. Nor is an institution, e.g., a cattery, a fun place to be when your folks are out of town. "Safely at home" means finding the right cat-sitter.

PICKING THE PERFECT CAT-SITTER

It's hard to get good help these days. It probably always was. Cat-sitting is not something to entrust to the kid down the block or to some entrepreneur who happened to find enough loose change under the cushions on the couch to run an ad in the Yellow Pages. Cat-sitters must be chosen with as much care as a French chef chooses vegetables, but without the squeezing part.

Your best bet is to select someone you know personally, such as a sister or mother, providing this person is (*a*) sane;

(*b*) doesn't bear a grudge against you; and (*c*) likes and understands cats.

Coworkers only enter the running if you have been to their homes and like how they interact with their own cat(s). The home visit is necessary, because your colleagues might be geniuses at, say, accounting, and charming at the water cooler, but could still let Tiddles out of the screen door on Day One and not have the nerve to summon you off the beach. Goodbye, Tiddles.

Let us regard the outside sitter. I don't say professional sitter, because sitter services are not usually regulated or bonded, not that such pacifiers would amount to much. Sadly, there is usually no knowing if sitters are truly experienced, trained, perceptive, or can actually differentiate between a cat in the pink of health and one with the heaves. This is not to say there aren't great sitters out there, but placing your trust in the innate goodness of humankind is not an appropriate response when leaving your cat's life in unfamiliar hands.

If you must use an outside sitter, here are some basic rules to follow:

1. A big smile is not a reliable reference. Check references *carefully* (try to determine if the folks providing the glowing endorsements are actually the sitter's relatives and friends).

2. Call the Better Business Bureau, your local Chamber of Commerce, and any and all animal protection organizations within thirty miles to ask if they have ever had a complaint about the sitter.

3. Meet the sitter in advance and ask her questions about cats and their care (wrong answers, wrong sitter).

4. Sign a contract, but not one that exempts the sitter from liability in the case of kitty illness, accident, or death.

5. Make sure the sitter agrees to check in with you every day, no matter where you are.

6. Leave your telephone numbers, those of your best cat-aware friend or relative, and that of your vet taped to the telephone.

7. Leave water in bowls in many rooms of the house (if the sitter is struck by lightning, causing your house key to melt, kitty is in far greater danger of dehydration than of starving to death).

8. Have someone you know and who knows cats check on the cat at least every two days.

9. Worry! This can help you think of other precautions.

THE ONLY WAY TO FLY

Charles A. Lindbergh was once asked why he had not taken his beloved kitten, Patsy, along to keep him company on his 1927 historic transatlantic flight. He answered, "It's too dangerous a journey to risk a cat's life."

Since cats don't have wings, there is only one right way to fly a cat.

Reuben, a dearly loved young tomcat, learned this lesson the hard way, when his people popped him into a plastic carrier, handed him over the counter to KLM officials, and walked trustingly out of the airport. Reuben found himself on a conveyor belt bound for the belly of a jumbo jet parked at the gate on a far-away continent. Although the tag on his cage read, DESTINATION: USA, he never made it. To this day, no one knows, or is telling, what became of Reuben.

Regrettably, Reuben's story is not even close to unique. Cats and dogs sent as cargo commonly arrive injured, traumatized, dead, or not at all. They suffer heat stroke or freeze when heating and cooling systems fail. They are crushed when cargo shifts during turbulence, and are even run over by baggage conveyors. There is no one to console them when your airbus behaves like a ski jumper during heavy turbulence.

What *is* unusual is the story of Tabitha, a tabby cat who was lost aboard a Tower Airlines 747 flight from Los Angeles to New York in 1993. At PETA, we were contacted to help rescue her.

Somehow, Tabitha had escaped from her carrier: another frequent cause of missing cats. Perhaps the latch was faulty or a traumatized Tabitha managed to find a way to squeeze out. Although the disappearance could have taken place during loading or unloading, Christa Carl, a psychic called in by Tabitha's family, didn't think so. She had a vision of Tabitha squashed up inside the metal paneling in the plane's cargo hold. Carl believed Tabitha was staying alive by licking drops of water which had condensed from a pipe in the cargo bay wall.

Airline officials, knowing their company would lose hundreds of thousands of dollars if they grounded the 747 for a thorough search, refused to do so.

It took twelve agonizing days before People for the Ethical Treatment of Animals and attorney Donald David managed to come close enough to getting a court order against the airline to persuade company executives to let a search party onto the plane.

Meanwhile, the plane had been in the air between San Juan, Miami, New York, and Los Angeles many times, logging in over 32,000 miles! Jimmy the Greek would have given a thousand to one odds on finding Tabitha alive.

Within seconds of Christa Carl entering the cargo bay, she pointed to the *exact* spot where Tabitha was hidden—frightened, thin, but alive!

Tabitha's airline horror story is the one in a million with a happy ending. Tabitha's owner, Carol Ann Timmel, is so happy that she has written a children's picture book about the saga, called *Tabitha, the Fabulous Flying Feline* (Walker & Co.).

On a more down-to-earth note, no cash settlement can replace a treasured family member, but in the case of animals hurt, killed, or "misplaced" during flight, families are never awarded damages of any significance: The courts have ruled that their lives are worth no more than the value of a Samsonite suitcase.

In fact, the way some animals are thrown about and otherwise abused by airline companies, they might as well be the luggage you see dropped out of the plane in those endurance test ads.

Imagine the agony of the people who had animals aboard a jet that crashed in Denver some years back. Humane officers couldn't persuade, cajole, or bully airport or carrier officials to let them inside the plane to rescue animals trapped in the cargo section of the wreckage until days after the crash!

One last point: According to retired Federal Aviation

Association officer Jim Wippert, all commercial aircraft cargo holds must either have a fire warning/extinguishing system or limit the air flow into the cargo hold. The theory behind limiting air flow is that a fire would soon use up all the oxygen in the hold and extinguish itself. Because fire-extinguishing systems are expensive and heavy and require continuous maintenance, most aircraft manufacturers prefer to use the limited-air-flow method.

In other words, the amount of air going into a hold is limited by design. An animal in the hold has a limited amount of oxygen to breathe. When the oxygen is gone, so are the animals. It happens. The airlines don't like to talk about it, and most airline personnel are not aware of this design requirement.

My advice for carrying pets in an aircraft is to carry them in the cabin.

The moral of the Tabitha and Reuben stories is this: The *only* way to fly a cat is inside the cabin, with you or someone you trust. All the tea in China couldn't make up for the loss of your cat, so even if you have to take out a loan to fly another human along, do it or you may hate yourself forever and be justified in doing so.

Most airlines allow at least one animal per cabin, some no more than one, so book well in advance. For international flights, a government-certified health certificate is required for re-entry into the United States, and you will need to check for quarantine restrictions, which vary from country to country.

For travel within the United States, all that is usually required is a certificate from your veterinarian showing that your cat has a current rabies vaccination, but always double-check with the airline and the state health department to avoid surprises on the big day.

Sturdy, heavy plastic, crush-resistant, regulation cat flight carriers are available at pet supply stores and from the airlines. They fit perfectly under the seat in front of you. During the flight, although you should *never* open the carrier door for fear of an escape, you can reassure kitty that the ugly sound of that jet engine and those horrible bumps are really hundreds of little mice feet beating on the floor as the mice run away, whispering, "Ooooh, a cat!"

Here are some other dos and don'ts:

1. Always try to book a direct, nonstop flight. Transfers just add hazard potential.

2. Don't fly during extremely hot or cold weather if you can avoid it; in summer, choose cooler night flights.

3. If your cat is high-strung, you may wish to administer a tranquilizer, but be vigilant—if kitty conks out, be sure she doesn't drift off, face down with her nose buried in the traveling towel. There is the danger of suffocation.

4. Do not feed or give water one hour or less before flight time. Try to time feeding and drinking so that your cat has done both *and* urinated and defecated before boarding (you may be able to place a tiny foil litter tray in the carrier).

5. Never leave the carrier unattended for even a moment. It's a crazy world, and even babies get stolen from hospital cribs.

6. Always be sure that both cat and cat carrier are very clearly marked with your name and the telephone numbers

where you can be reached. It never hurts to add the words REWARD IF FOUND. Motives are unimportant when you and kitty are desperate to find each other.

GETTING KITTY INTO THE CARRIER

Sounds simple, doesn't it! If kitty is comatose, it is; or if your cat is used to sleeping in the carrier or finding a cache of favorite treats hidden inside it. But if kitty is halfway functional and only used to going to the vet in that thing, getting her into the carrier without losing clawmark-size parts of your shoulder is as simple as making something edible out of garden mulch. You will have to call on your powers of persuasion and, possibly, deceit.

Because cats can see, don't parade about with carrier in hand or get it noisily out of the closet. Subtlety and speed are called for here. Plan your maneuver carefully first. And don't smile too much. The cat's no fool. Try to act as if nothing's up.

1. Make sure the carrier bottom is comfy, not lumpy, barren, cold (don't store it in the potting shed), or lined with thin paper. A warm towel makes a good floor covering.

2. Make sure the door works well and closes tightly. If necessary, oil the hinges. There may be a time and place for fumbling, but as on a date, this isn't it.

3. Try to ever-so-quietly get the carrier as near as possible to the cat without the cat seeing it. This means that once you pick the cat up, there isn't far to go. Keep the carrier at chest level (yours) so that you don't have to bend down at a crucial moment.

4. Pick Tiddles up, facing *away* from the carrier and, talking gently to her so that she will never trust you again, move backward if necessary, until you are just in front of the carrier.

5. Back her into the carrier, gently but firmly. Before you let go, keep one hand inside the carrier at her face level to stop her from dashing out as energetically as she would if given a clear view of the escape hatch.

6. Slip a little treat in through the bars.

7. Latch. Cover carrier with a towel. Pick carrier up evenly (some people seem to instantly forget there's a cat onboard and start swinging it about, banging it into doors, holding it at weird angles, and otherwise misbehaving).

8. Depart. Do not be tempted, for any reason, to open the carrier until you are safely shut in a room somewhere.

There. Easy wasn't it?

GETTING KITTY INTO THE CAR

Dogs may drool out of the window, bark at bicyclists, and snort the air as it rushes past, but they are not cats. Cats regard even slow-moving vehicles in much the same way claustrophobics view closets. If you multiply by six million that teeny bit of skepticism you once entertained about the structural integrity of an old bridge or how well your car would do if you accidentally flipped it over, you will have some idea of how comfortable most cats are with motorized transport. Even the horn scares and disgusts them.

A lot of this is probably attributed to the fact that the only time most cats see the inside of a car is when their next sight will be the inside of a veterinarian's office. Cars mean something unpleasant is getting even closer.

Some cats were introduced to car rides for pure fun in their kittenhood and seem to actually enjoy them. Once in a blue moon, you see some show-off driving along with a cat draped over his shoulder. This does not alter the fact that cats and cars are a bad mix.

For example, if a vehicle backfires, a gun-shy dog may cower, but a cat will flee (in strange territory, chances of recovery are slim). George, one of the most dearly loved cats ever to grace a household, was lost in this way.

George was en route to the vet when it happened. As he was lifted out of the car and into his "dad's" arms, a trash truck turned on the grinder. George must have thought a monster was about to snatch him into its jaws. He fled for his life, leaving deep claw marks in the arms of the man who tried to stop his escape. Ads in the paper, cards left on veterinarians' bulletin boards, enquiries, all came to nought. Whatever became of George we do not know.

Cars also have windows and seats. While it may be impossible for a wolfhound or even a corgi to clamber out through a tiny crack in the window that lets the driver pay a gas station attendant or a toll, most cats can squeeze their way out of a toothpaste tube. As for seats, I have never heard of a dog getting caught in the springs under a seat or having to be cut out of the metalwork over the wheelbase, but both things frequently happen to cats. Extricating them wastes a chunk of a person's life and sometimes a chunk out of the car. The cat may emerge physically intact but can suffer emotional scars that never heal.

If you are going to put a tiger in your Taurus, here's how to do it right:

1. *Always* use a sturdy carrier. Double check that the carrier door is absolutely secure. *Never* let your cat loose in the car. PETA's Alison Green says, "If, for any reason, you find yourself in a car with an unrestrained cat, don't ever, ever, ever open the door or window until you have the situation completely under control. Countless cats have been lost at tollbooths and rest stops this way."

2. Keep the carrier from wobbling by creating as flat an area as possible for it to sit on (pack a towel around the outside if you need to). Do not let Tiddles see that she is headed for the car—drape a breathable cloth over the carrier before heading out the door, place the carrier on the flat space in the car, then rearrange the cloth so that she can see you, if possible, but not out any window. The sight of the earth or sky speeding past causes most cats to panic, begin open-mouthed breathing, howl miserably, and contemplate suicide at the next stoplight.

3. Pad the inside of the carrier with something comfy, like a towel, to make travel easier by preventing bumps.

4. Play the radio softly to drown out traffic noises (try a soothing classical music station).

5. Talk to your cat as you go. If she complains, always answer reassuringly. (Here's an actual, sample conversation. Comment: "Meow!!!" Response, "It's all right. I know." Question: "Meoooooow!!" Response, "Sweetie, I know. I know.")

6. Remember how frightened you are when you get into

the car with your oldest relative, now retired to Florida, at the wheel? Don't drive that way. Avoid lurching forward, brake smoothly, and imagine you are delivering crystal glassware that will shatter if you do not look ahead and steer clear of manhole covers.

7. When you arrive at your destination, let kitty scope out the new indoor setting from the sanctity of her carrier, then offer her food, water, and litter outside it. In strange surroundings, ensure that all doors and windows are shut as tight as can be before even one whisker emerges from that carrier.

ROOM AT THE INN?

Although almost every guesthouse, hotel, and motel in the world allows even the most ill-mannered human child through its portals without so much as a peep, someone with an absolutely impeccably behaved cat can find the door slammed in her face.

Pets-R-Permitted is a travel directory of establishments that do allow cats and includes information on National Parks and their pet policies. Some charge a small extra fee; some require a refundable damage deposit; others are totally animal-discrimination free. Order it from Annenberg Communications, P.O. Box 3930, Torrance, CA 90510-3930 or call 310-374-6246.

Another good directory is *Vacationing with Your Pet! Eileen's Directory of Pet-Friendly Lodging,* by Eileen Barish, Pet-Friendly Publications, P.O. Box 8459, Scottsdale, AZ 85252 (800-496-2665), $19.95, 688 pages. Over 20,000 listings.

You can also try *Take Your Pet USA: A Guide of Accommo-*

dations for Pets and Their Owners, by Artco Publishing, 12 Channel Street, Boston, MA 02210 (800-255-8038). A solid list of hotels and resorts where your cat is welcome, plus good advice, such as information on quarantine restrictions in Hawaii (which may soon be modified or abolished).

Hotels that score extra points for being cat friendly:

- Hotel/motel chains that allow animals include Holiday Inn, Best Western, Comfort Inn, Motel 6, and Super 8.
- Four Seasons Hotels allow animals worldwide. Some restrictions apply and vary from hotel to hotel. Call 800-332-3442 for information about a specific hotel.
- Loew's L'enfant Plaza, Washington, D.C., and Loew's Annapolis Hotel, Annapolis, Maryland, have a VIP (Very Important Pet) policy. Five percent of their room rate charge is donated to a humane society. Companion animals at Chicago's Inn at University Village get water, food, and treats delivered to the room. Other classy animal-loving accommodations include New York's Hotel Pierre and Los Angeles' Hotel Bel-Air.

> TRAVEL TIP: In case of emergency or accident, take along your cat's health records. To help a cat feel more at home and adjust quicker, throw his toys and bedding into your luggage, too.

10

Where, Oh Where, Can My Kitty Be?

This chapter could save your cat's life.

One way not to lose things would be to thread a string through every single thing you own. When something goes missing, all you have to do is follow the string. Sadly, this doesn't work for nonthings, like cats. If it did, this chapter would not so bluntly proclaim the horror of a missing cat.

Although there are few deeds that beat rescuing someone from danger for securing their undying love, admiration, and even hero-worship, there are easier ways to curry favor. If your cat disappears, you will have to earn your detective degree and hero status on the superfast track. It's no good trusting that your cat will be like miraculous Camila, a cat who found her way home by walking 125 miles through Portugal. Something untoward can easily happen. Every minute counts, or kitty could end up somewhere decidedly unsavory: upside down on a hospital table "advancing the cause of science," or flat as a pancake on the freeway.

Of course, as with most ordeals, an ounce of prevention is worth a pound of cure, especially since some conditions, such as rigor mortis, are incurable.

This means keeping tabs on kitty from the moment you make him your own, always securing doors and windows and only letting your cat out with a chaperon or in a secure enclosure.

It means being wary of messengers, visitors, children, and other careless souls who don't realize that a vigilant feline can drive a freight train through a crack in a screen door and could get as far as the Yukon by nightfall (read "New York" if you actually live in the Yukon).

It means taking a set of good pictures of kitty now, just in case, and making sure kitty is always well dressed, i.e., wearing a clearly readable, current tag. The collar must be detachable to prevent your cat from hanging himself (it happens) and immediately replaced should it vanish. Buy in bulk.

Kitty should also be tattooed. I advise against using your social security number, which isn't readily traceable, and suggest instead using a phone number, including area code, of course. If you are a gypsy, in the military, too young to be settled, contemplating divorce, or have nomadic tendencies, make it some settled person's number, perhaps that of a parent. Don't forget to let whomever it is know this and keep reminders coming, at least twice a year. If the tattoo doesn't work in reuniting you with your cat, it may at least deter some scalpel-wielding vivisector. Ask your local humane society or veterinarian where to find a good cat tattoo artist. Despite what ship's cats and sailors may say, tattooing does hurt. However, your cat will have his skin desensitized, unlike human subjects, some of whom routinely keel over and meet Mr. Floor out of sheer fright.

Microchip implants are catching on, but only a few progressive shelters use this system and the special scanning equipment it requires; and you can be relatively certain someone about to carve into your kitty for science or pleasure won't check for a chip. However, you might ask your vet where to get this simple injection for your cat or call Schering Plough Corporation at 908-298-4000. The company markets systems called AVID and Home Again. Just don't use it as the sole I.D. method.

Don't think for a moment that your cat can't or won't leave home, given half a chance. It's not that a cat wants to walk away forever; it's just that even a harmless little stroll can turn into a lifetime loss. Snow and rain can mask or obliterate the vital scents that lead kitty home. An interesting excursion into a drain or culvert can become a nightmare when a sudden surge of water blocks escape. Accidents happen, and as clever as cats are, even they are no match for foul play.

Some members of our own species, called "bunchers," make a living from setting traps for cats or even netting them straight off the street for resale to laboratories. Some years ago, the prestigious Mayo Clinic in Minnesota was found harboring seven of thirteen dearly loved animal companions, all stolen from farm homes in a nearby county.

Cats are used for everything from live training tools for pit bull dogs to shark bait in Hawaii. In England and Russia, and even in South Dakota, cat fur has been found used as trim on coats.

And, yes, Virginia, there truly are wanna-be satanic cults,

sometimes composed of teenagers who derive desperately sought feelings of power from torturing cats. In Florida, whole blocks of cats have disappeared around All Hallows Eve, or Halloween. In Sacramento, the organs and entrails of cats have been found arranged in symbolic ways on people's lawns.

Finally, there are few things worse than never knowing what became of someone you love, not knowing if they are dead or alive, and if they died, how.

So, always keep the apple of your eye well in view, safely at home with you, and then you can use this chapter to line kitty's litterbox.

MOOMIN'S TALE

I lost Moomin, the little Siamese kitten I described in the introduction to this book, when she was in her middle years. It happened because of my carelessness.

It was summer, peak theft season. I had a reception to attend; my air conditioning was broken; and it was hot. I left my bedroom window open just a few inches, trying to capture the breeze and push some of that muggy Washington air out the way it came in.

When I got back to the house that night, Moomin was nowhere to be found. I called and called and walked the yard with a flashlight. Nothing.

The next morning, my panic rising, I combed the bushes, searched neighbors' yards, talked to the mailman, but had no luck. By nightfall, I was beside myself with worry.

I did everything you will find listed in this chapter, and I did it all twice. By the tenth day, I felt as if my heart had been crushed by a steamroller. Where was she? Was she alive or dead? How could I have allowed something to happen to such a vulnerable little cat?

A friend suggested I call a psychic. I thought the idea was absurd, but at that point I would have tied oranges to my ears and stood on my head if someone had suggested it might bring Moomin home.

I reached the psychic by phone. She told me not to recount any circumstances surrounding the disappearance, but to express my feelings and to describe my beloved cat. That was tough. Tears streamed down my cheeks and my voice broke up as I traced Moomin's face in my mind and said how much I loved her.

At some point, the psychic said, "Let me tell you what happened." I put every thread of skepticism aside to listen.

Moomin, she said, had "left through a window when it was dark, walked down a few steps, and crossed a very big road directly outside your house. It was very quiet and she felt adventurous, so she started to explore in a field on the other side of the road.

"When it started to rain, she hid under some bushes. Later, the rain stopped. She returned to the road, but, by this time, it was light and everything had changed. The road was full of cars. Moomin was too frightened to cross back. She heard you calling, but she couldn't come to you."

I was stunned. Moomin *had* left by the window. There *is* a small set of steps near it. Outside my house there *was* a six-lane highway: a commuter route that was quiet at night, but chock-full of traffic by morning. It *had* rained in the early hours of that morning, ten days earlier.

The psychic was in California and had no idea I was calling from Maryland. I had no idea what to make of this, but I kept quiet and listened to what she had to say.

"Moomin is tired and scared," she continued, "but she's still alive." The woman believed my little cat was across the road, living under a house, eating out of bowls of food left for other cats. She wished me luck and refused payment.

I was out of the house and across the road in a flash, walking among the houses, calling and calling until dark. Again, nothing. It had all been rubbish. Moomin was nowhere to be found. What more could I do? I was desolate.

The next day, the phone rang. The caller had seen one of my big, plyboard signs at a nearby intersection.

"I've been trying to decide whether to call or not," she said. "I think your cat is living under my porch, eating out of my cat's dish. I've been thinking of keeping her."

The caller lived almost a mile away, straight through the field on the other side of my street.

Moomin lay on my bed that night while I sat watching her, feeling happy as happy can be. She was very thin, very dirty, extremely hungry, and totally exhausted. She had gulped the food I gave her, then, most uncharacteristically, fallen asleep without cleaning herself. For the first time in her life, her ears twitched at every sound and she woke many times until I assured her that her return was not merely a dream.

I imagined how frightened she must have been, seeking refuge under that house every night, living on scraps; she could only have been startled by raccoons and opossums, not knowing which humans were friend, which foe. How she must have longed for her home and hoped for those she loved to come and rescue her.

I knew how lucky we had both been. How close I had come to losing her forever, psychic or no psychic. I knew I would never be so foolish as to let Moomin or any other cat out of my sight again.

STEP-BY-STEP RECOVERY PLAN

If kitty goes on the lam, you will need to move like the wind, by which I do not mean whirl about quickly and purposelessly. Luck is great, timing is important, but organization is everything.

HERE ARE THE BASIC RULES:

1. No matter what your commitments may be at work, they can wait. The material world isn't as important as your cat's life. Recruit relatives to look after the kids. Tear up your dance card, postpone your wedding. Take emergency leave. Do whatever it takes to free yourself up.

2. Beg, borrow, steal, or charge an answering machine so that the number you are about to plaster up everywhere is always answered.

No matter who else you are expecting to hear from, no one is more important than the person who has found your cat or has a lead to his whereabouts. Record a new phone message along these lines: "Please, don't hang up if you have information about my missing cat. I must speak to you. If you can leave your name and number, please do so, twice, speaking very clearly, at the sound of the tone. If you do not have a number, this phone should be answered by a live person between x and y today, or you can reach (someone else you absolutely trust) at (another number you are absolutely sure of). Your call is vital to me. If I do not call you back, it means your number didn't record clearly. Please let me talk to you. Thank you."

3. Find out which humane societies and animal control agencies exist in your area. Don't assume there are only one or two. Ask each place you call, "Where else should I check?" then ask again and ask every time you call. Different people give you different leads. Check yellow pages; ask veterinary hospital receptionists; call pet shops; and ask the sheriff's office dispatch clerk.

4. Visit each shelter every day *no matter how often they assure you that they will call you if kitty shows up.* Lots of called-in and turned-in animals go unrecognized or ignored in busy shelters.

Ask to see the Lost and Found book. Be pleasant but persistent. You need these people, but—very quietly, in your own head—assume they are, at worst, incompetent or, at best, too busy to be relied upon. I love most shelter workers, and if your cat's life is on the line, you will need help from them; but saving your cat's life means never relying completely on anyone other than yourself.

5. Make clear copies of the best photo of your cat you can find (try a one-hour processing place or use a copy machine if you have to). Ask that a copy be glued or taped into the Lost Book in every shelter and put one on every bulletin board.

6. Call all local papers and run an ad. Say only, "Lost. Cat. (Whatever) color. Reward. Phone Number." Don't mention kitty's gender or breed (if any), haircoat length, or other confusing details. Most people couldn't sex an elephant accurately, let alone a cat, and their idea of breeds would make a show judge weep. You won't want to miss that

all-important call because Mr. Finder thinks your calico girl is a neutered Himalayan boy. If necessary, keep running the ad until the paper goes out of business. Check the Lost *and* the Found ads in it daily. People at newspapers sometimes mix the ads up.

7. Don't chintz on the reward. How much could you rustle up for emergency surgery if you needed to or if your roof sprung a leak? You are not tipping a waiter, you are trying to lure people who otherwise would not give a hoot into finding your irreplaceable angel. Cough up.

8. Try to get local radio and television stations to run an announcement for you. If there is something catchy about your cat that might engage their interest, mention it. For example, if your infant child can't sleep since kitty's been missing; if your cat has just arrived from Minnesota and may be trying to hoof it back there; anything quirky or cute might win him a life-and-death mention.

9. Strip-search the neighborhood:

    a) Talk to mail carriers, delivery people, and folks you haven't uttered a word to, or wanted to, in years.

    b) Bribe children; they hear and see more than adults.

    c) Use a flashlight to peer into gullies and drains, parked cars, and toolsheds.

    d) Go out at night and call your cat's name when all is quiet. Listen carefully for the faint "meow" of a cat stuck backward down a standpipe. For the first time in your life, you'll find yourself wishing cats barked. Don't forget that cats get stuck inside small spaces in walls and vehicles and can't extricate themselves.

10. Salvage or buy some giant pieces of plywood. Spray paint your simple, standard message on them:

BIG REWARD
LOST CAT
COLOR
RELIABLE PHONE NUMBER

11. Put flyers in vets' offices in case your cat has been injured or taken ill. Drop them into storm doors in the area, and put posters on telephone poles. *Cover a Large Radius.* Many cats are found one to two miles away.

12. Call a pet-locating service for advice. Petfinders, Inc. has been in business for twenty-one years and can be reached at 800-223-4747. Locating services will also register animals and send their information to shelters for you. In Defense of Animals also has a pet-theft hotline and some nice information. They can be reached by phone at (415)388-9641 or by fax at (415)388-0388.

13. Post a notice on the World Wide Web. This is not to say you should hold out any great hopes, but never leave a stone unturned. The Agriculture Department's Animal and Plant Health Inspection Service displays pictures scanned from ordinary photographs and lists lost and found animals by state. The site can be found at http://www.aphis.usda. gov/reac/anlost.html.

14. You have the legal right to visit laboratories and dealers to look for your friend. Contact them quickly!

15. Follow any and all leads and do anything anyone suggests. Light a candle for Saint Jude if you feel like it. Who knows what will bring kitty home?

Most important, never, ever give up, and look *everywhere*. Cats have been found locked inside a soda machine recently serviced by a mechanic, trapped inside the wheel of a private jet, and even inside a Mercedes shipped by sea in a crate nailed shut and bound for Europe. I once united a family with their dog, Blossom, after five months. Their daughter had raised Blossom from puppyhood, then dropped Blossom off at her parents' home for some reason. She didn't speak dog well enough to be able to explain to Blossom what was going on, and Blossom didn't understand. Seizing an open door opportunity one morning, Blossom set off to reunite herself with the daughter. Who knows what happened, but when I found her, Blossom was living like a tramp, holed up in a culvert along an interstate. Her coat was full of sticks and clumps of dirt, and she had been hit by a car.

Whether the daughter ever realized how she had let Blossom down, I have no idea. But I do know how pleased the parents were to see Blossom and how delighted Blossom was to see them again.

One final word. *The Incredible Journey* is not something you can count on. Very few cats or other animals can prevail when trying to trek home. It happens, and over thousands of miles, but the odds are stacked against mere cats in this harsh, mechanized, auto-filled world.

11

Excuse Me, Do You Speak "Cat"?

Human beings can be such supremacists! For decades, scientists solemnly gave lectures in which they declared that what separates man from beast is that only humans use language. After a while, sensible people started giving the scientists some well-deserved raised eyebrows. Today, according to a study conducted by Alan Beck, 99 percent of pet owners report talking to the animals they live with, and 75 percent of children say they confide in the animals they love.

It's not a one-way street. The fact is that most, perhaps all, animals use forms of language, even if we can't understand or recognize them as such. Elephants, for example, communicate at frequencies too low for us to hear. Ethologists eavesdropping on elephants in the African bush used to pick up strange low rumbling sounds on their sophisticated microphones and think the pachyderms were peckish. Eventually they put two and two together.

As for cats, they can hear sounds at frequencies of 65,000

cycles per second or more, which is inconvenient for mice who commonly squeak at that frequency. Cats can also hear sounds more than two octaves higher than the highest note we can hear.

Behaviorists (clearly a group with too much time on its hands and someone else footing the bill) have also learned that birds speak different dialects, depending on the region in which they grow up. Observers taped the sounds of crows in the south of France and played them back to crows in northern France. The crows in the north went, "Huh?" They hadn't a clue what the other crows were crowing about. Of course, in the wine regions, perhaps none of the crows can understand what the others are saying after a few beakfulls of delicious champagne grapes.

Chimpanzees cannot speak, because their vocal cords aren't constructed in the same way ours are, but they readily learn American Sign Language and even make up their own words. One chimpanzee, called Washoe, signed "water" and "fruit" when she tasted her first watermelon. When she doesn't like something her keeper does, she swears at him, signing "you dirty toilet."

The list of interspecies communications we have managed to figure out is long. For example, marine biologists believe that whales actually sing their histories as human tribal peoples do, passing information down through the generations, each year changing part of their elaborate song to mark new events. We know that tiny prairie dogs have a vast repertoire of language. They not only warn each other of pending intrusion, but can use different sounds to convey what species the intruder belongs to, whether he or she is familiar, and what the intruder's intentions seem to be.

(Prairie dogs even use *adjectives*!) Their language apparently goes something like this: One prairie dog to another, "There's that skinny fella from the Prudential again. He's got a trainee with him. Get in your burrows or they'll try to sell you insurance."

Many scientists who study cetaceans (whales and dolphins) believe our language studies with dolphins have failed because these big-brained beings "talk" too fast for us to keep up; their signals are too sophisticated for us to interpret; and dolphins may in fact communicate in whole pictures, in much the way we receive television transmissions!

As if that weren't weird enough, consider this: Even that fly on the wall may be telling other flies what he's seen. The human ear can only differentiate gaps between a hundred words a minute. More than that sounds like. . . a buzz!

The communication patterns of bees are legendary—their dances are highly detailed and purposeful.

If all the other reasons to forgo dissection in school weren't enough, frogs communicate by sending vibrations through leaves and clicking out messages with their toes, much like Morse code.

It's a wonderful world.

WHAT WE HAVE HERE IS A FAILURE TO COMMUNICATE

Since we're not smart enough to learn "cat," cats often find other ways to communicate with us. Some are less than satisfactory. Take Lisa Lange's cat, Camila, who sticks a claw up Lisa's nostril every morning to let her know it's breakfast time.

Most cats have more important things to do than teach us how to purr fluently, so how *can* we break the language barrier?

First, the don'ts.

Someone once said, "If I tell my dog, 'Come here,' he runs right over with a 'Yes, what can I do for you?' look. The cat's response is 'Put it in writing and I may get back to you.'" That's because cats know a thing or two.

Some people let that creepy old word, "Master," go to their heads. They consider the way to communicate with an animal is by giving orders. You've seen certain people with their dogs. All they seem to do is issue commands. It's "Sit, Max," "Here, Max," "Be quiet, Max," "Max, down. I said 'Down!' Max," "Heel!" "No!" "Come." Their dogs must lie awake nights wondering who signed them up for the Marine Corps. What a life!

Other people whine in a high-pitched voice as if their animals are totally demented. "Ooooh, the itty bitty goopie schmoopie. . . ." Even Attila the Hun probably appreciated a bit of baby talk once in a while, and being schmaltzed beats being bossed about, but cats have dignity and presence. That glint in their eye probably means, "If you don't stop that, I'm going to give you back my breakfast!"

If you must let your cat know that some behavior or other displeases you, try hissing or blowing a puff of air into his/her face—that's what mom would do. You may also spit (or use a spitting surrogate, such as a plant mister) if the situation gets out of hand. Never throw anything, strike the animal, use your hand to discipline them, or make a very loud noise or you may create lifetime loathing.

Hopeless optimists try to read human words into cat

sounds. I was in someone's living room once when she grabbed me by the arm, pointed to her cat, who had just very distinctly said "Meow," and whispered, "Did you hear that? She said, 'Mama!' " There was nothing to do but nod energetically, then suddenly remember that I had left the oven on at home. Wishful interpretations can prevent us from accepting that cats simply don't care to learn our language. They have a perfectly good one of their own. Just because Berlitz hasn't marketed the six-week course in it doesn't mean we can't learn to speak "cat."

The Eyes Have It

It's lucky we're dealing with cats, not cuttlefish. Cuttlefish, or squid, are amazing, complex invertebrates who communicate by flashing waves, blotches, and circles of ever-changing color over their bodies. To touch base with a squid, you'd have to wear a suit something like a plug-in Christmas tree.

One major way cats communicate is by using their eyes. This is helpful because we have eyes, too.

Cats' eyes are not exactly like ours, however. Experimenters at the University of Oregon in Eugene and other bastions of great learning have wasted vats of federal funds and countless cat lives trying to put to human use knowledge gained from interfering with cats' eye movements. It can't be done.

According to veterinary ophthalmologist, Dr. Ned Buyukmihci, "Humans have a very specialized region in their retina with which they see and almost all their vision depends on that specialized area. Cats don't have that specialized area. Also, cats have a much greater ability to see at night. These and other reasons make the information from vision experiments on cats worthless if it is to be applied to humans."

Veterinarian H. Ellen Whiteley reports that cats can see in light only one-fifth as bright as the faintest light we can see and that their complex ears contain thirty different muscles, whereas ours have only six. But no set of figures or charts can convey the anger, annoyance, bliss, love, and subtler emotions your cat's extraordinarily expressive eyes hold. So don't think I was scrimping on design costs when I left out the chart.

Cats' pupils dilate when they are angry or on the attack, and cats smile at us and other cat friends with appreciative eyes by squinting.

Your cat will slowly, almost, but usually not quite, close her eyes and reopen them while looking at you. When almost closed, the eyes are held at the lowest point for a second. You can return the sentiment by gently squinting back, mimicking the cat's pattern. It would be rude to do anything less.

If a cat closes her eyes all the way for more than a split second, that is absolute trust in action.

If your cat "smiles" when looking at you, you are observing a private contentment, expressed publicly in the same way you might give a happy sigh in an empty room.

To read eyes, you have to watch closely.

When your cat sees a bird outside the window and that tail starts twitching, compare the look in your cat's eyes to the look that accompanies a different tail-twitching experience—the appearance of a strange cat. Although your cat's eyes will dart back and forth in both cases, the first look is reserved for interest in prey, the second for interest in a potential marauder. Although the two looks are different to the seasoned cat observer, both hold elements of annoyance, keen interest, an awareness of the potential for action, reserve, and the need for vigilance.

Annoyance is commonly expressed in joint eye and tail action. If you are not attentive, you can get swatted at or bitten, simply because you missed your cat's polite warning that he or she was in no mood to be petted or picked up.

BODY LANGUAGE

Kittens who were weaned too early, or who just plain miss their mothers or the pleasant sensation of nursing, knead at the air with their feet as if still pumping milk out of their mama's chest. If they chose you to do that to, what a high compliment indeed.

Cats in cages at the animal shelter flatten their ears back in fear or as a warning, call out plaintively, and frantically push their paws through the bars. Some bat at people passing by, appealing to them in the same way any prisoner might. In less desperate surroundings—your kitchen, for instance—cats may paw at you to let you know it is past suppertime and your watch has stopped. It is rude to ignore being batted, so even if the cause of the swat is not immediately apparent, try to figure it out.

Your cat sends messages by stretching and yawning. Of course, tense cats don't do either. Chances are, your cat feels wonderfully contented if she throws back her head, bends her spine, extends her legs, and unwinds with a yawn. Let her enjoy the feeling without being moved, asked to play, or called to a meal.

Lions and tigers and the smallest of small cats also stretch to show off to others of their kind or to predators. Such stretches can mean, "I'm so in control here, I can relax." The show of teeth that accompanies yawning can mean, "See these? Pretty big, eh! So don't try to take advantage."

Grooming is carried out for practical reasons, of course, but also to cover embarrassment. When a cat does something that doesn't quite work, like jumping up to catch a moth and missing, she will immediately sit down and start vigorously cleaning a limb.

It's as if your cat is saying, "That klutsie-seeming thing you just saw was actually quite purposeful. I was about to catch that fly when I remembered some grooming that needed to be done and, look, here I am doing it now." Even if kitty does something extraordinarily silly, never laugh! Laughter is indeed a universally understood language.

THEREIN HANGS A TAIL

The cat's tail is perhaps his most expressive body bit. When you could play jumprope with its thrashing movements, watch out! But there are few sights more pleasing than kitty walking toward you with a big question mark tail or making featherlike figure-eight rubs between your ankles. How joy can kink a tail like that, no one knows! Cats would make terrible poker players. Every time they got a good hand, their tails would bend like a shepherd's crook.

Slow thumping is a warning, "Look out. I'm annoyed!" Fast swishing is annoyance sitting on the springboard, ready to turn to full-fledged anger. A twitch is like a doubletake, neither cat nor tail knows at the moment of the twitch what will happen next.

One of PETA's rescued cats, Jack, spent his first year confined to a cat crate in an eccentric person's home. Now he has the run of the office, but can often be found sitting, waiting for me by the elevator when I've run out to an appointment. As soon as I step out, Jack flips over onto his back, and I must resist the urge to ruin the moment by rubbing his beautiful tiger tummy. Instead, I touch his head and say "What an angel, Jack!" happy in the knowledge that sad cats never roll on their backs.

What a treat it is to see cats lie upside down and bump their rumps from side to side. I think it means they have just won the lottery. I always check in the cat bed for a winning stub.

Swapping Gifts

A few years ago, a Las Vegas animal trainer named Bobby Berosini was found locking his performing orangutans alone in solid, stainless steel boxes between acts. The boxes were barely bigger than were the animals themselves, with no windows and only tiny airholes at the tops.

The apes came to know that this man had the power to take them out of the box, as well as seal them away from the world and each other. Berosini permitted no one else to feed the orangutans. Small wonder that, when he let them out of their prisons, they hugged him. They saw him as not only their jailer, but as their ticket to sustenance, even life itself.

Sadly, Berosini's mean treatment of the orangs illustrates that all living beings will show gratitude to those who feed them, whether or not that person is decent and loving or exploitative and rotten.

In a loving home, cats wish to return the favor. They don't just take. They try to reciprocate. Cats who go outdoors may go to enormous trouble to bring home prey—alive, dead, sometimes in bits—to present to their beloved; the head is the cat equivalent of picking out something very, very special for you from the Neiman Marcus catalog. This unwanted treasure must not go unappreciated.

Wrong response: "Jees, will you get that thing away from me!"

Right response: "Ooooooh, thank you," followed by much appreciative petting. Then read chapter 14 and lock the door.

In the wild, protocol would demand that you eat a bit of the body first, then allow the gift-giver a chance to share some. This is not recommended unless you are prepared to pump your stomach and dose yourself with worm medicine.

It would be incredibly rude to be seen to dispose of the gift quickly or in front of the giver. Here's the protocol:

If the animal is dead, try to show your appreciation by batting the body, or body bit, about. If the animal is alive or if you cannot bear to take my first suggestion, withdraw with the offering into a closed room. This will allow you to examine the body for injuries, effect release through a door or window, call a wildlife worker, or just mull things over. Kitty will assume you have sought a private place in which to admire and guard your treasure.

Dealing with these delicate situations provides yet another reason to keep kitty safely in your home with you, rather than out there in the wild blue yonder, shopping for his or her adopted parent. (See chapter 14.)

MESSY MESSAGES

Cats, being mortal, physical, and emotional beings, can get jealous, sad, and ill. Sometimes, people don't notice. This forces the cats to resort to drastic measures to get their point across. Witness an article in *New York* Magazine entitled "Is Your Cat Contemplating Suicide?" which asks, "Are New York's cats neurotic, dysfunctional, or just plain screwed up?" Many city cats, according to the article, are in the same sorry shape as Gus, a bear at the Central Park Zoo, who had gone mad from boredom and stress and started to swim obsessively back and forth in his tiny pool. Now, Gus is on Prozac (really!) and has professional help and toys.

In my experience, it's not just city cats. Let's take a look:

Say you have recently moved, taken up going to the gym every Saturday, or divorced. Perhaps there is a new baby in the house or a visiting dog. Could it be you spend most evenings gazing, enraptured, into the eyes of a new Mr. or Ms. Right? Don't think your resident feline isn't affected. Even a new perfume can throw kitty for a loop. If you no longer smell like you (a big deal for sensitive, scent-oriented beings), who knows what's sacred (or safe) anymore? Sadness; worry; separation anxiety; insecurity; or fits of out-right, downright pique may dominate his or her mood.

Some cats, particularly if they have other cats in the household, can force themselves to tolerate your new love or take your frequent absences in stride just as your old flame may be able to play tennis with your new love without smashing Beau Number 2 with the racquet. One change that is more than any cat can take, however, is to find himself no longer allowed on the bed. Your cat believes, as did the ancient Egyptian cats, that a cat's duty is to guard you, the most cherished object of his love, from attack during your most vulnerable time.

Sometimes, a cat is reduced to making a truly desperate cry for help. This can take the form of urine or feces left on the table, the bed, or in some other spot guaranteed to capture your attention. Even a neutered male may start spraying urine on furniture. This is not an accident or a sign of stupidity or poor training. It can be a communication to you from a cat who felt you were not listening.

Cats suffering from cystitis—bladder or urinary tract infections, all of which can be very painful and even life-threatening—tend to urinate in odd places, sometimes particularly on a ceramic or tile surface, such as in the bath or sink. You may or may not see blood in the urine. Please, *rush* your cat straight to the vet for treatment. Every painful moment counts.

Such a physical outpouring of emotional anguish should not cause you to concentrate on changing the cat's behavior, but on modifying your own. Your cat could be telling you that he is physically ill and needs emergency assistance (see above) or feels left out, betrayed, scorned, miserable over the loss of another person or species, abandoned. If it is the latter, you must be convincing in showing that you still feel the same love and affection for him you always did and that he still holds a most special place in your heart. Punishment has no place here.

If that means arranging that special dinner for two at your home, rather than going to a restaurant, or inviting the team over to watch sports videos instead of always hitting the courts, don't waiver. You made a commitment to your cat first.

Introduce your new love, whether baby or boyfriend, to your cat *now*, no matter how long all this has been going on. Kitty needs to see that you are proud of him, so stroke and praise your cat in front of the new love.

Most cats can, if begrudgingly, accept that you are so weak-willed and emotionally needy that you may seek another source of affection. What is totally unforgivable is for you to lavish attention on someone else *to the exclusion* of your cat.

Never, never, allow yourself or a friend to push your cat off the couch or bed or to say words equivalent to "go away," even during the most amorous moments. Respectfully work around your cat until your cat decides to go away of his own accord, no matter how long it takes. You don't want your cat to go around with a chip the size of Mount Rushmore on his shoulder.

Cat Got Your Tongue?

Hank Ketchum said, "Meow is like Aloha. It can mean anything." Most of us who recognize the basics of cat lingo would disagree with Mr. Ketchum. There is the long, mournful call of the lonely young female; the spitting sounds of the fighting male; the chirpy half purr, half mew that greets your home-coming; and the scream of pain when a paw accidentally gets underfoot. It's the rich language of more subtle conveyance in between that escapes us.

Answering back, even if you get it wrong, is usually appreciated. Any return sound means, "I hear you. I am responding." Best of all, if kitty understands your language as little as you understand "cat," she may think the miscom-munication is all on her side and blame herself. Oh dear!

Cat photographer Elizabeth Cyran believes cats use methods of communication of a higher order than we are able to understand. Says Elizabeth, "Look at the pictures alien abductees draw of the aliens. They are cats! They sig-nal the mother ship late at night. They know things we don't. They communicate without words. I vowed I would never share my life with a cat. They were nasty, clawed the furniture and smelled. Now I know how wrong I have been. Life without a cat is no life!"

Well, whether or not cats are communicating in other ways, cat sounds can be heard with the ear and the heart. Enjoy the music of the sound and sing back. I have had long conversations with some of the cats who have shared my home and have yet to be committed. If they hear you respond, they will invariably try something back, and on it goes. You are like musicians "spelling" each other in alter-nate riffs, cooperating, in touch, even if each keeps his own tune.

Talking back is especially helpful to your cat if she is call-ing out in distress, panic, or worry, perhaps stuck on a high ledge or in the car on the way to the vet. Your answer says, "I am here. It's going to be all right." Your words will have the same reassuring effect the rescue worker's voice has on a person trapped in a collapsed building. Whether or not everything will turn out all right may be anyone's guess, but for the moment you can provide comfort and calm your cat down.

Contrary to the opinion of Barbara Holland, someone quoted as saying, "By and large, people who enjoy teaching animals to do things will find themselves happier with a dog," respectful interaction with a cat can be as beneficial to the cat as to the human being initiating the lesson.

Use the same sentences consistently and often. If you have a special way of announcing food or a supervised walk, your cat will not so much become used to the words, but to the length and sound and tone of the sentence. Listen to yourself when you talk about routine events, then try the same words in the same tone and feeling, but in a different place and without other signals. If you can evoke the right response, e.g., your cat jumps up to speed into the kitchen, although you've said, "Let's see what's for dinner," in the *den* and without touching the can opener, you're on the right track. Develop one, then two, then more key communicative sentences and see how it goes.

Here's something for extra credit: *Finding Your Inner Purr* is the name of an audio cassette, subtitled "The Cat Lover's Guide to Relaxation." Newspaper reviewer Wendy Christensen relates that when she played the tape for the second time, Dandelion, one of her cats, "seemed to pay unusually close attention, . . . snuggling up next to me near the stereo speaker, something she rarely does. This twenty-pound wild

cat look-alike with a temperament to match seemed pro-
gressively more mellow as the tape played, especially side
two, 'Purring With Your Cat.' " Christensen felt silly doing
it, but bravely followed the directions, breathing and purring
along with the narrator. She reports that Dandelion, who is
usually unreceptive (the nice term) to having her triple-
thick, easily matted fur groomed, was so relaxed that she
purred as Christensen worked a comb through it.

The sixty-minute tape is available for $12.90 from
Imaginer Communications, Inc., Cherokee Station, P.O. Box
20721, New York, NY 10021-0074 (800-949-0688).

PROFESSIONAL HELP

Anyone can teach a cat not to jump on the counter (put citrus deodorant spray, double-sided sticky tape or plain old
water on it until kitty hangs it up) or a kitten how to use his
litterbox (place him in there gently and work his front paws
in a scratching motion). But if your cat develops behaviors
that you cannot figure out and cannot live with, perhaps it's
time to consult a cat behaviorist. Be sure the one you pick
from the yellow pages is certified, not certifiable. There are
some dangerous, know-nothing shingle-hangers out there.

Of course, certification *guarantees* nothing, but it does
mean the consultant has passed either an associate course in

TOP TIP: Check out the training books in
the recommended reading list at the end of
this book.

applied animal behavior or, better, is an applied animal behaviorist. It also means the consultant is supposed to abide by ethical standards imposed by the Animal Behavior Society.

Only a few dozen such behaviorists have expertise in cat stuff (not the technical term). Ask for references, as with any veterinarian, and check with your local Better Business Bureau and animal protection organizations to see if anyone has lodged complaints about the consultant.

Most important, walk out if they seem impatient with the patient or suggest anything you wouldn't do to yourself.

12

Is Your Angel
Suffering in Silence?

If ever domesticated cats manage to get a Bill of Basic Rights through Congress—and I wouldn't put it past them to do so one day—the right to decent health care could top the list of their entitlements. It would appear directly above a cat's inalienable right not to be moved from your lap, even though he has somehow been magically transformed into a fifty-pound lump that has cut off all circulation in your legs.

Who can concentrate on love when they feel awful? You know what I mean if you've ever tried to have a conversation with someone with a pounding headache. They are utterly incapable of concentrating on anything other than their burning desire to have you stop talking and go somewhere else. Your cat's the same way.

Perhaps one of the very worst things that can happen to a cat besides falling asleep in the clothes dryer (yes, this happens—see chapter 15) is that no one notices that he has developed a physical problem.

It's hard to imagine cats as the strong, silent type given that they can yowl up a storm if someone steps on a body part. However, like most wild animals, who are aware that predators put you on their dance cards if you announce your vulnerability, they tend to clam up rather than cry out when they are in a bad way.

What happens if *you* wake up with a toothache, develop a ten-ton headache, or suffer from arthritis? Unless you are a Navy S.E.A.L. on active maneuvers, it is a safe bet that you will promptly seek relief. But what if you couldn't? Put yourself in your cat's paws. Imagine being in pain and discovering that no one notices and that you have no way of communicating your condition to them.

Because pain is invisible, a mental event, this can be the frightening reality cats face when things go quietly, physically wrong for them.

Take Roger, a handsome, neutered male cat, who lived with my friend Kim. Roger developed a nasty disposition. He no longer enjoyed being petted, and sometimes he hissed at Kim or even scratched him when Kim rubbed his head affectionately. He had become totally intolerant of the family dog and of visitors. Kim attributed this impatience to age and simply complained back to his cat.

One day, Kim had to take Roger to the vet for a routine immunization. He happened to moan to the vet that his cat had become a grumpy old man. The vet asked a few questions, then put Roger on the clinic floor to test his ability to find his way about. The old cat didn't do very well.

Now Kim was no ordinary cat owner. He was a veteran animal rights campaigner who had spent all his adult life trying to help animals. You can imagine how chagrined he felt when the vet announced that Roger had been seriously ill for a long time. He suspected that there was a tumor growing on Roger's brain.

In fact, the tumor was causing problems with Roger's vision, but because the cat knew every twist and turn in his home, Kim hadn't noticed anything wrong. The pressure from the tumor also caused Roger considerable pain, especially when anyone touched his head or neck. That is why he hissed, moved away, and when people were persistent, even bit or scratched. His pathetic acts of self-defense had been mistaken for nastiness and had been met with disappointment and reprimands.

Something more common, but even more dangerous, happened to Humphrey, a cat who lived with Diana, a lawyer friend of mine.

Diana had been working hard on an important case, staying at the office until very late at night, then dashing back to work again as soon as she could get out of bed in the mornings.

She had simply not been around enough to notice that Humphrey had started to use the litterbox frequently. She wasn't there to see that he sometimes returned to the box within a few minutes of his last visit, or to hear his tiny, reserved "mew" when he strained to urinate. She hadn't had time to play with him or notice the new, pained expression on his face.

Every morning, Diana carefully dumped the contents of Humphrey's litter pan into a bag and refilled the tray. She noticed nothing because the litter absorbed the evidence of Humphrey's distress.

Then, one morning, Diana jumped into the shower and

found tiny drops of bloody urine on the porcelain. Humphrey had found a way to let her know he was in trouble. Still, Diana didn't realize how deep that trouble was. Calling from her office, she made an appointment to take Humphrey to the vet the next day, not suspecting for a moment that Humphrey was in agony, his urethra blocked.

The next morning, when Diana walked into the bathroom, she found Humphrey lying motionless on the floor. He had gone into shock. His painful bladder infection, which can afflict male and female cats alike, had caused systemic poisoning. Despite immediate surgery, Humphrey did not pull through.

Within the week, a far more vigilant Diana noticed her other cat, Rayette, straining to pass urine. This time Diana was on the way to the vet within minutes. Her cat had cystitis, which sometimes goes through a household of felines, and Diana's immediate response spared Rayette any of Humphrey's pain, as well as her life.

Sometimes serious illness can escape even the most conscientious souls, like Kim. When you hear yourself say, "Isn't he well-behaved today?" or "Doesn't that cat sleep a lot!" or "Boy, he doesn't usually do *that*!" you could be noticing that your cat is run down, weak, not feeling very well, unable to move about comfortably, or otherwise in distress.

Any change in a cat's pattern of behavior or mood merits some thought and a closer look right away.

I recommend doing the following every day (not because you really need to do it that often, but because your cat will love it):

1. Run your hand slowly from stem to stern along kitty's body, feeling gently for lumps and bumps, seeing if your cat appears sensitive to the touch anywhere, parting the hair to check for fleas, hair loss, an ear infection, you name it. This is the kitty equivalent of getting a back rub every day and will bond your cat to you like glue.

2. Look into your cats' eyes. Don't forget to blink adoringly or your cat will think you have gone off the deep end. Are the eyes weepy? Is the skin inside the eye at the inner corner covering part of the eye, rather than being almost imperceptible and flat? That is your cat's nictitating membrane, and it may be trying to tell you that kitty is under the weather and that further investigation is in order.

3. Very gently pull back the skin around kitty's gums (while rubbing his face for fun) and see how those teeth are doing. Do they need cleaning? (If so, see chapter 4.) If the gums are white or very pale, your cat could be parasitized.

4. Sniff kitty's breath. Is that home cooking or is something rotten?

5. Sneak a peak under kitty's tail. This is a delicate maneuver that can cause deep, lasting offense, so take it easy. It may work to incorporate the under-tail inspection into some serious rump scratching, which will make your cat raise his tail. Is everything clean and shipshape? Or are there surprises, e.g., a prolapsed rectum (the skin has popped out and is distended) or the sort of untidiness that can mean parasitism or an upset tummy?

6. Squeeze each toe very, very gently, until the nails come out and you can look for breakages or abnormalities.

7. Look (and smell) inside ears. If you see gunk, put a

tiny bit of mineral oil on a cotton swab and wipe gently. If those black dots move or jump, you'll need ear mite medicine. These mites particularly annoy the owner of the ear. We know this because a human researcher actually placed cat ear mites in his own ears just to see how things went. He woke up with a start at 3 A.M. every morning as the mites got an early and vigorous start to their day! To deal with them you will have to very gently dig all around your cat's cavernous, convoluted ears, and that is a big job. Infection greets your nose with a little zing and requires analysis before a remedy can be chosen. If your cat digs in an ear or two or shakes his head a lot, there could be a problem that deserves attention.

8. Rub your fingers lightly under and between your cat's paw pads in case a Spanish doubloon or prickly object is uncomfortably lodged there and could lead to infection.

9. Look at kitty's haircoat. See if it is shiny (not greasy, which is a sign of ill health) and has elasticity, i.e., if you take up a fold of skin on kitty's back and then let go, it knows where it is supposed to be and springs right back where it belongs. If the skin "sits there" or very slowly returns to take its place as part of the greater cat body, your cat may be dehydrated. Is that automatic water dispenser clogged (throw it out anyway in favor of a stainless steel bowl you can clean and fill daily with fresh water) or could your cat be suffering from diarrhea? If the coat is dull, perhaps kitty is parasitized and needs a stool sample dropped off at the vet's. If the coat is dry, perhaps your angel's diet would benefit from more fresh, steamed vegetables (see chapter 16) and a drop of vegetable oil, like olive oil.

Bathing a cat's outside bits will not restore a cat's inside bits, so look for the cause before choosing the cure.

10. Brush away excess hair with any effective brush from a pet supply store or catalog. Most cats prefer plastic (like Sheds-All, the "professional tool," available from RAF Trading Corp, 101 Albany Avenue, Freeport, NY 11520) to metal—there's something scary about steel. Perhaps it reminds cats of ships.

If you don't brush, cats can ingest wads of hair when they lick their coats clean. Hair balls may make good material for stand-up comics, but they aren't digestible and can clog up a

TOP TIP: Be sure you conduct your cat exam with enough light to let you see what you are doing.

TIP FOR THE GERIATRIC CAT: Elderly cats can suffer joint pain and feel the damp in the same way oldtimers like to tell you they know it's going to rain. They may not be as agile in their dotage, either, so we must not only keep them warm and shield them from drafts, which can whip along like Hurricane Agnes at floor level, but we must be sure they have cozy bedding they can reach without using mountaineering gear. A bed with sides, either store-bought or fashioned from a cardboard box filled with soft material, does the trick, especially if it is at about chair seat level.

A CARDINAL RULE: When it comes to your beloved's health, there are two good slogans to adopt: "Better safe than sorry," and "Rather a vet than a regret." If in doubt as to your cat's condition, call. If a telephone chat with the vet or the vet's assistant doesn't satisfy you or solve the problem, make an appointment. If the condition is any more serious than a hangnail, do not put off the visit for even a day. Go to the emergency clinic if your regular vet is closed. Just ask yourself, if it were you, would you wait? And if your vet isn't helpful, don't hesitate to get a different one.

cat's innards, causing nasty, knotty problems. One sign of them: Your cat stretches his neck out, crouches low to the ground, and coughs, usually with little to no result. Your vet can give you a malty-tasting lubricant that will help, but routine brushing and a good diet works just as well for most cats.

13

One Kitty Too Many: Uncomfortable Decisions

One hopes you will never have cause to use this chapter, but cats happen and, sadly, it is not always possible to offer a permanent home to every one who crosses your path. Cats descend on some people with the regularity of birthdays, which seem to come more and more often these days. My mother believes that some of us have a VACANCY sign on our doors that can be seen only by people and animals who are down on their luck. Unlike motel signs, we can't change it to FULL.

One bitter winter day, many years ago, not the sort of weather you want to change a tire in, I was driving along a country road, my mind completely uncluttered with thoughts of cats. I wasn't on my way to meet the pope, but I did have an appointment that was scheduled to begin at a particular time as appointments usually do. Of course, such commitments mean nothing to a cat.

The road I was on had been plowed after a severe snowstorm, but beyond the asphalt, every field and bush was covered in ice. The temperature was in the teens, and the wind blew wafer-thin sheets of snow and ice onto the car as I drove along.

I was flicking the wipers on and off, trying to push off the icy muck splatting up against my windshield, when I noticed that, at the very edge of the road, the all-encompassing whiteness had been interrupted for a split second by a tiny flash of orange and black. I tawt I taw a . . . guinea pig?

Braking cautiously on this skating rink of a road, I stopped the car and backed up until I saw that flash of colors again. There was a ball of fluff, certainly the size of a guinea pig and with the same long, coarse hair in the same colors as a guinea pig, but not a guinea pig at all.

When I stopped, the ball unwound itself to become a tiny kitten. I opened the car door and leaned over to scoop her up. She didn't run. I don't think she could have. Her little body was doing the jitterbug so hard from the cold that I could actually hear her teeth rattle. Her whiskers were covered with ice and little icicle tears ran from her eyes down to her chin. Her long calico coat was blowing like a polar bear's coat in the bitter wind.

"Mew," she said, in the angry, anxious, pitiful voice of a desperate, betrayed little being. She glared and pleaded at the same time as if to say, "Please save me. This is a very cruel joke, and I do not wish to be part of it any more, do you understand?"

As small as she was, I felt pretty small myself. After all, it was one of *my* kind who had chucked this vulnerable little kitten out into the freezing tundra in the middle of nowhere and then gone back to somewhere warm. Aargh!

That was in the Days of Yore, before mobile phones, so back we went to my house to cancel the appointment and crank up the heat. Soon, "Campus" was fast asleep, curled up between the pillows on my bed, toasty-warm and well fed, having wolfed the equivalent of her own body weight in vittles. All the other cats were barred from entry and sat in a big cat heap, outside the door, pouting like a dozen Brigitte Bardots.

Campus did get to stay, but I knew that the next cat through the door could not. There really was no room left at my inn, unless I sacrificed the mental health and physical well-being of the rest of the troupe. Overcrowding leads to stress. The "I'm tired of being a small fish in a big pond" syndrome impacts on a cat's immune system, and respiratory viruses, cystitis, and other health problems have less trouble getting their foot through kitty's door. Other options had to be explored.

Finding the right home for a needy cat is harder than convincing Charleton Heston to become a Democrat. With Heston you'd have to be tough, but with cat placement you have to be tougher. You have to soak your resolve in 3-in-1 Oil. That's because the words "I'll take that cat" do not guarantee a good home, and "I promise to give him a good home" can be a promise not worth the paper it isn't written on.

I can't adopt a positive Julie Andrews-like frame of mind on all this, because my experience as a humane officer has made me realistic. If compassionate people could see what eventually becomes of so many of their well-intentioned placements, they would realize finding a truly good and lasting home is a bit like searching for the Holy Grail. My advice is to make a promise to yourself that you will never risk your cat's happiness by settling for anything less than a home you are *sure* is excellent.

If the prospective adopter cannot satisfy all the requirements outlined in *Guidelines for the Sale or Giveaway of Your Cat* (see page 69), taking kitty to a *good* shelter (see below) is a safer option. It may be a horrible fact, but a fact nonetheless.

Again, taking kitty to a decently run shelter where she'll have a chance of a good placement or at least a kind end, is far better for the cat than foisting that unwanted feline onto a casual taker.

The old Chinese proverb contends that if you save a person's life, you are responsible for it. Well, if you save nine lives, the same responsibility applies. A bad home—where kitty's pain may go unnoticed, where she is left vulnerable to passing cars and delinquents, and where she becomes a kitten breeding machine, churning out offspring in a world where so many go homeless—is *not* better than going to heaven or that great void in the sky.

Do cats have souls? Well, there is no final authority here to ask, so opinions differ. If you think they do, then death cannot be such a horrid fate, especially for the innocent victim of unprovoked meanness. If you think cats do not have souls, then all the more reason to make sure every moment they spend in this, their *only* life, is pure joy. If we ourselves cannot give them happiness, they deserve a wonderful placement or, at least, a ticket off the planet.

FINDING THE RIGHT HOME
FOR YOUR CAT

You care about this cat, and you want to find him a good home. But remember, not every inquirer will share your understanding and concerns. The following will provide the information you need to select a good home and help ensure that the cat you place will still be cared for next year and even eighteen or twenty years from now.

BEFORE YOU MAKE THAT
BIG DECISION

Are you reluctant to part with an old or, for that matter, a new friend but feel you have no choice? Be sure you explore all your options before taking the big step. Once an animal leaves your care, can you be absolutely certain he will be safe and treated well for the rest of his life?

If your cat is having behavior problems, consult a veterinarian first to make sure illness isn't the root cause. If he is given a clean bill of health, try a behaviorist or humane trainer. Don't hesitate to call local humane groups or PETA for advice!

Having financial difficulties or traveling for an extended period of time? Ask a family member or trusted friend to care for your cat temporarily. Also, humane and breed rescue groups may agree to foster your friend.

Having trouble finding an apartment that allows animals? Try networking through local humane societies and animal rights groups. Post ads in veterinarians' offices, companion animal supply stores, and health food stores. Beg your prospective landlord to make an exception: Evoke testimony as to your goodness from previous landlords, add an extra deposit, even offer to wash your landlord's car on weekends. Show off a photo of your cat(s) looking enormously humble and cute, very small and totally harmless—much the way you might behave in front of the judge at traffic court. If you are threatened with eviction over a companion animal, the Animal Legal Defense Fund (127 4th Street, Petaluma, CA 94952, 707-769-7771) may be able to help.

Allergies?

- Have someone who is not allergic brush the cat every few days.
- Run a warm, damp cloth over your cat's coat every few days to pick up extra dander.
- Change your furnace and air filters often, choosing the finest possible mesh recommended by the manufacturer to keep dander from floating about in circulated air.
- Wash anything you can as often as you can.
- Avoid shag or high-pile carpeting.
- Get a "fresh air machine," a good quality air purifier that removes cat dander and other bits and bobs from your atmosphere. There are lots of models, available by mail order from XL-15 Air Purification, 1404 Hickory Heights Drive, Waverly, IA 50677 (319-352-4191) or enquire at your local pet supply store.

Guidelines for the Sale or Giveaway of Your Cat

Here are some basic questions designed to give you necessary information about a potential adopter's attitude and level of responsibility.

"Why do you want a cat?"

Look for someone who wants an animal to be part of the family as a household companion. Beware of anyone who may want a cat, especially a purebred, for breeding. They want money, not a cat. If someone wants the cat as a gift for a friend or relative, insist that the person who will spend the next decade or more with the cat be involved in the selection. No cat or any other animal should be a surprise gift. The surprise may be that the recipient doesn't want the cat, and the cat finds himself resented or homeless again. If a child calls, ask to speak with his parents.

"Have you had cats before? What happened to them?"

People who have never had cats before should be advised of the considerable expense and responsibility involved in caring for them, including exercise, feed bills, and veterinary costs. Someone who has had several animals stolen, killed by cars, lost, or given away is undoubtedly a poor prospect and should be summarily dismissed from consideration.

"If you move or travel, what will happen?"

Caring for a cat can be a twenty-year (or more) commitment. Remind prospects that they will have to make arrangements for someone to care for the cat during vacations and must

plan for the animal's needs if contemplating a move. Ask
what arrangements will be made in those circumstances.

"WILL YOU ALLOW THE CAT OUTDOORS?"

This is a trick question. If the answer is yes, unless you gen-
uinely believe in the power of instant reeducation of adults,
don't trust the cat to be safe on the streets.

"HOW DO YOU FEEL ABOUT SPAYING/NEUTERING?"

More than 20 million animals are destroyed each year
because there are simply not enough homes to go around.
Always require that the prospective owner pay to spay or
neuter *before* adoption to avoid further breeding, resulting in
more homeless animals. (Veterinarians can now spay and
neuter kittens when they are just eight weeks old.) If you or
the prospect are concerned about neutering costs, call your
local humane organization to find out about reduced fee pro-
grams. Be cautious if people already have an unaltered animal in their home: They may have breeding in mind.

"DO YOU OWN OR RENT YOUR HOME?"

If the prospect does not own, see if her lease permits cats.
Thousands of animals are given up each year after being discovered by the owner of the property. Just because everyone
is violating the rules doesn't mean that the boom won't drop
on all the animals whose people are getting away with it now.

"WHO ELSE LIVES IN YOUR HOME?"

Make certain all other members of the household want a cat
and are aware of the caller's plans. Also, determine the ages
of any children in the household. Families with young chil-

dren should be told that normal kitten and cat play behavior often includes jumping, kicking, and biting and that cats must be protected from rambunctious children.

WHAT TO DO IF YOU ARE UNABLE TO FIND THAT GOOD HOME

Please don't rush into a placement because you are pressured by time. If you are unable to find an *excellent* home for your cat, take him or her to an animal shelter operated by a humane organization. Choose a shelter that (*a*) checks out prospective homes carefully by doing home checks; (*b*) requires spaying or neutering; (*c*) does not give or sell animals to research institutions; and (*d*) if euthanasia becomes necessary, uses a painless sodium pentobarbital injection intravenously (just as good veterinarians do).

A humane death is far better than a cruel, slow death by disease, exposure, starvation, or being crushed under the wheels of a car, and better than a life made hellish by negligence or cruelty. A peaceful end is certainly preferable to the lives so many animals lead—turned out into the street or locked up in a bathroom, garage, or basement where fresh air, proper food, clean water, exercise, regular health care, companionship, respect, and love are in short supply.

If your animal friend is old, very shy, or dependent on you, and you cannot find a home with someone he trusts and loves, the kindest course may lie in taking him to a veterinarian or shelter to be euthanized. Animals who have been with you a long time may suffer and pine terribly when you are gone. When I went to Ireland for four months leaving my beloved Jarvis with my best friend, he wouldn't speak to me for about as many months as I had been gone. He obviously thought I'd deserted him, that I simply didn't care. Cats may have short attention spans but they have long memories. Their hearts break just as ours do.

As a final kindness, remain in the room to comfort your old friend during euthanasia.

Never sell or give a cat or kitten to a pet shop. People operating pet shops are obviously concerned with running a profit-making business and often have no concern whatsoever about what happens to animals after they leave the store. Without a thorough screening process, kittens are sold to people buying on impulse and to people who are unfit to care for an animal. When Kim Novak cradled a Siamese cat in her arms in the movie *Bell, Book and Candle,* Siamese cat sales soared only to be followed by a huge Siamese cat influx at pounds and shelters.

WARNING!

There are people who acquire cats to sell to laboratories. These folks are often quite cunning and pretend to seek animals as family companions. They may bring children or senior citizens with them to gain your confidence. In Los Angeles, Bob and Elsie Anderson lived at the desert's edge. Soon after moving there, they discovered people using the desert as a favorite dumping ground for unwanted animals.

Bob and Elsie found the courage to go into the desert and retrieve these animals in various stages of deterioration, pull the cactus needles from their paws and noses, make expensive and inconvenient trips to the vet, and with unfailing mercy, they returned these animals' lives to them.

Eleven cats and nine dogs later, the Andersons realized their home had reached its carrying capacity. They didn't stop rescuing animals, but rather than take them off to the pound, they chose instead to find them homes by placing giveaway ads in the newspaper.

Enter now Mrs. Pierce, a nice little old lady, who explained to Elsie that her husband had died recently, and she very much wanted a dog to keep her company. Before relinquishing the dog to Mrs. Pierce, Elsie requested visitation rights. Of course she could visit the dog, Mrs. Pierce replied.

A week passed before Elsie called to ask how things were going. The dog is fine, she was told. After a few more days Elsie made her first visit. Mrs. Pierce wasn't home, but one of her neighbors was, and when Elsie stopped to chat with him, she traveled that difficult path from the sheltered world of innocence to the grim realities of experience. From that conversation she learned that Mrs. Pierce's son, a dealer registered with the United States Department of Agriculture (USDA), earns his living selling cats and dogs to laboratories.

Bob and Elsie took their case to every authority they could think of, hoping to find someone who would help them get their dog back. No one took an interest. In sheer desperation, Elsie and Bob went down the list of giveaway ads in the paper and called every person who had entered one. They found fourteen people who had delivered animals into the hands of Mrs. Pierce, including one woman who released two cats—a mother and her daughter, both recently spayed, on the grounds that they would not be separated.

With renewed determination, the Andersons resumed their search for help. Finally, they found a USDA official who agreed to look for the animals. Of the fourteen, he found four. One was dead. The other three, Tippy, Spike, and Duke, were found in holding areas still waiting for laboratory assignment. The vocal cords of all three were severed. Teeth on both sides of young Tippy's mouth were knocked out, undoubtedly as a result of rough handling during the debarking procedure. Their experience left the three of them psychologically scarred; the slow progress back to health would demand a saintly patience and consistent, hard work on the part of those caring for them. Furthermore, their physical condition was a disgrace. You could count every bone in their bodies and their nostrils were caked with mucus.

The moral of the story: *Don't think this can't happen to you or the cat whose future you hold in your hands.*

Always ask for identification (legitimate callers will not object when you tell them why). Write down the person's full name and driver's license number and explain that you will visit her home (to ensure that she actually lives there and, yes, you actually will do this). Ask for (and check) references from veterinarians, neighbors, and employers. Most important, if you are advertising your animal in the newspaper, never say, "Free to a good home," the favorite five words of "bunchers" (middlemen who sell animals to laboratories).

Before taking out any newspaper ad, consider putting up photos and ads at veterinary offices and animal supply stores and hooking up with local animal rescue groups. Names of rescue groups are usually available from the local shelter. To find purebred rescue groups near you, look in the Project BREED (Breed Rescue Efforts and Education Directory) directory at your local library or order a copy from Project Breed Animal Rescue at 202-244-0065.

Finally, always charge a fee. If the adopter cannot now afford to cover the cost of neutering, for example, where will this precious cat end up if he requires serious medical care later?

ADOPTION CHECKLIST

- Visit the prospective adopter's home. Ask to meet the other members of the family and observe their reactions to the animal. Be wary of the parent who says, "Johnny will be responsible for the cat," since this could mean that no one will provide regular care or the animal will be given away when Johnny loses interest. Never feel pressured to leave the animal there!
- Make sure the adopter understands the basics of responsible animal care, including ID tags, veterinary care, leashes, and fences for dogs. Stipulations, such as spaying or neutering, need to be put in writing and signed by the adopter (see sample agreement).
- *Don't hand over your cat until you are completely satisfied.* If you have any doubts about the adopter or the potential new home, or if the situation feels wrong in any way, don't be afraid to say "no" or "let me think about it." Your cat friend's happiness and life depend on it.
- To ease the transition, send along toys, leashes, collars, harnesses, scratching posts, and carriers. Books and leaflets on cat care are also helpful.
- Leave your name, address, and home and work phone numbers and urge adopters to call if they have any questions or problems. After the adoption, make at least one unannounced trip to the new home to make sure the cat is happy and well cared for.

SECURITY

Be sure the cat is wearing a collar and an I.D. tag with your number and the number of the new owner. Write the owner's name, phone number, and address on the outside of the collar in indelible ink. Tattooing or microchipping your cat before release can also help protect him and ensure recovery in the event he is ever lost or stolen. Advise the new owner not to leave the cat unattended at first; a sense of belonging takes time to develop. A cat who has never before urinated indoors, hid under furniture, or hissed at the family may do so in strange surroundings or when stressed or pining.

BE KIND TO YOUR LOCAL SHELTER

As a caring person you will probably be upset to hear that, in just one week at any large shelter, roughly the same number of people you could find at a ballgame dispose of their cats as casually as they might toss out a paper cup. The difference is that they accompany the deed with these eight little words: "You won't put him to sleep, will you?" This utterance allows them to step out of the door again, into the sunlight, and get on with their busy lives having nicely shifted the burden of guilt from themselves to the poor slob at the animal intake desk. Shelters staff are often the innocent whipping boys for society's major shortcomings in the "how to care for animals" category. So, if you must, please be kind to the people with the difficult and thankless job.

HOW TO FIND A DECENT SHELTER

Leave nothing to trust. Call first, then if you get the right answers, go visit. Sans the cat. You do not want to be talked into leaving a nice kitty in a nasty place.

Here's what to ask:

1. *What do you require of a new adopter?* Do not accept less than a shelter that requires:

a) Spay/neuter, preferably *before* the cat is released. (Of course, if *you* can accomplish this before passing kitty on, that would be very helpful, but be sure kitty has enough recovery time before entering a shelter, where he may be vulnerable to viruses from other cats.)

b) A preadoption home check

c) The adopter to pay for shots, sterilization (if not already performed), and an adoption fee. If the adopter cannot afford these start-up expenses, will kitty find himself thumbing a ride to the vet from the curb when he suddenly needs an expensive (is there any other kind?) operation?

d) Adopters to sign a contract, allowing the shelter to reclaim the cat if the home is not suitable and prohibiting declawing or allowing the cat to go outside without supervision.

e) That, if the adopter lives in an apartment, the adopter's apartment lease allows cats. If it does not, kitty may have to walk the plank the next time the adopter's landlord comes a-knockin'.

2. *What is your policy on releasing animals to laboratories or dealers?*

This should be a clear, unequivocal "We don't." No waffling allowed. Some pounds and shelters still hand over cats to medical colleges for show-and-tell, hands-on courses or for long-term research into nausea, pain, and the workings of the eyes or brain (this means electrodes are implanted into the cat's skull). As one famous poster says, IT'S NOT THE CAT WHO NEEDS HER HEAD EXAMINED!

3. What method of euthanasia do you use?

The correct answer is "the intravenous (into the vein) injection of sodium pentobarbital." This method is absolutely painless and animals lose consciousness in two to three seconds. Other chemicals can cause discomfort or are downright painful and are, therefore, not acceptable.

If the person you are dealing with rattles off the brand name of a drug, ask, "Is that sodium pentobarbital or something else?" If it's "something else," express your disappointment and dial another facility.

If they say it is sodium pentobarbital, but don't mention how they administer it, ask. If the answer is "into the heart," try another facility.

4. Do you allow someone bringing in an animal for euthanasia to stay in the room with the animal?

Even though you are probably not planning to avail yourself of this service, the answer to such a question can help you judge the facility. The very best shelters actually encourage people to be with their animals when they receive that last shot. To be that open not only shows that staff has nothing to hide behind that back room door, but is good for the animal and his person. Having a loved one, not just strangers in the room, can calm an animal in distress, and the grieving human will always be able to look back and be comforted in the knowledge that everything went well during their beloved companion's last moments.

A few humane organizations run placement services. However, do not assume that they have given a blood, I.Q., or any other kind of test to the person whose name and phone number you may receive from them. In fact, some unscrupulous dealers may pose as loving candidates for your Ms. Tiddles through these caring folks' bona fide placement agency. Be prepared to put on your personal inspector's hat and do your own careful checking.

A Word about "No Kills"

"No-kill" shelters may sound like an attractive option, but because they do not euthanize animals except under extreme circumstances, beware! A very few of them are extremely good, but many others are houses of horror, Bates Motels for animals. Visit *without* your cat and look as well as listen, then ask yourself, "Is this *really* a safe and promising place for me to choose?" Because they must limit the number of animals they accept, most no-kill shelters take in only highly attractive, young, or purebred animals, turning away the neediest, such as the sick, the old, and the pregnant gangly mixed breed. Those end up at other facilities then forced to kill animals to make room for new arrivals.

At some no-kill shelters, "unplaceable" animals end up living in cages for years. They can become withdrawn, severely depressed, and "unhousebroken" and can acquire antisocial behaviors that further decrease their chances of being adopted. They are the living dead—sentenced to life imprisonment with no chance of parole and with no happy moments in the sun. If one cat in a cage of fifty gets cystitis, will anyone notice before it's too late? Well-meaning people who take on the huge physical and financial responsibilities of a no-kill shelter can find themselves overwhelmed very quickly, and too often the animals suffer from lack of individual care and attention. Some no-kill shelters have been shut down by humane officials after gradual neglect turned into blatant cruelty. Others simply hand animals over to any takers—without checking to ensure their wards do not end up in a laboratory or abused.

14

Don't Go Down to the End of the Town, Unless You Go Down with Me

If A. A. Milne had meant cats, not Christopher Robin, when he wrote those lines, he would definitely have been dispensing good advice. Never let your cat out without you, unless you have escape-proofed your yard. If that sounds over-the-top to you, Dr. David Epstein, a veterinarian in Glenview, Illinois, warns that "at least 85 percent" of the thousands of cats he has treated in his practice over a forty-year span are brought in by owners who let their cats roam free. Here is a partial list of what a cat misses by staying indoors, courtesy of the San Francisco SPCA:

- Fights with other cats
- Fights with dogs
- Fights with raccoons and skunks
- Infections from puncture wounds
- Gunshot wounds
- Thrown bottles or rocks

- Fleas, ticks, worms
- Being stolen
- Being hit by a car
- Feline Leukemia Virus
- Feline Immunodeficiency Virus
- Steeljaw leghold traps
- Rat bait poisoning
- Pesticide poisoning

I can vouch for the fact that this list is definitely partial. What I have seen happen to cats has scared me out of letting cats onto the street, ever.

Here is just a small taste: As a humane officer, I had the job of collecting the remains of a cat who had been ritually tortured and mutilated by juveniles who thought it was cool to play at being in a satanic cult. At another time, I picked up a cat whose head was full of metal staples put there with considerable ingenuity by a bored and sadistic transient. That cat lived, but another cat who wandered by a garden-floor apartment during a party didn't. It was no consolation to the cat that the court sentenced to jail the young man who did the deed. He had swung that poor cat repeatedly against the wall and then buried him, still breathing, in the woods behind the complex. I could go on, but as I say, the list is endless and depressing.

Of course, birds, insects, mice, and moles will miss your new indoor cat in the best of ways. The toll cats extract on free-living animals is phenomenal. It is conservatively estimated that, in the United States, 4.4 million songbirds are killed *daily* by cats. The number of tiny mammals like mice and rats is even higher. Imagine being captured by a great alien being with eyes the size of Volkswagens and claws like boathooks; think how your tiny heart would pound, and you will understand how those small animals feel.

For years, I was terribly stubborn about letting my cats out. Other people had horror stories, but nothing happened to *my* cats. They were smart. Then one of my littlest angels, Crystal, a cat I had always told people "never goes anywhere," disappeared.

I searched high and low, the panic of loss growing. How could she have vanished out of thin air? I *knew* she hadn't been hit by a car. After all, we lived on a cul-de-sac then, a slow road to nowhere where a few cars a day, not counting my neighbors', cruised along slowly, looking out at the river. Anyway, although tiny Crystal would have lost any argument with a 3,000 pound vehicle, she was so wily, so cautious, so clever.

Of course, she *had* been hit. Whether she had lain unconscious for two days or had been too weak to call out, I will never know. On the third day, she found the strength to drag herself home. She must have been so relieved to have made it all the way to the back steps. How long she lay there waiting for me before her end came, I don't know. I found her there when I came home from work. The vet said her lungs had collapsed and her ribs were broken on one side. I could see that she had lost a great deal of blood from the size of the gaping hole in her side. I was so angry with myself. I had loved Crystal so much, but I had so stupidly allowed my nonchalance to cause her such pain.

After that, we built a cat run of "non-climbable" fencing stretched over fence posts. Of course, cats being cats, they didn't take this gracefully at first. We had to contend with nasty looks, much screaming and clawing at the doors, and mad dashes through your legs if you dared to set a foot outside. Then they settled down. Of course, it would have been far simpler had they never been used to going outside.

We knocked out a small basement panel window and replaced it with a cat flap. Our cat "tribe" soon realized they could go through the flap at will, then play in the dirt, feel the breeze, even lounge about in the sun on a good day. We erected a haphazard structure of orange crates and stumps that allowed them to climb and jump and sun themselves or hide for private naps. This structure proved enormous fun and kept the cats agile and exercised, as well as amused. They invented their own version of "Who's the King of the Castle" and never seemed to tire of amicably lording it over each other.

When I moved into a city apartment, the run was scrapped, but by then I had found all sorts of ways to give my cats only the best of what they would experience outside, with none of the peril.

The modern world is far too dangerous a place for unattended, trusting little life forms. Today, I would no more open the door and say, "Go Play" to my cats anymore than I would to a toddler.

WHAT YOU CAN DO

1. The best news is that if you have a yard, or even a patio, you can effectively fence it to keep cats in. Cats can leap over, climb, or otherwise defeat standard dog-person fencing, so you will need cat-proof, keep-'em-down-on-the-farm, angle fencing.

You can do it yourself by erecting angle wire inward from your fence top or you can buy a special system, like Cat Fence-In. This is not an electric fence (which I do not recommend), but has a tangle-free net of small mesh that attaches to any existing wood, masonry, wire or chain-link fence. It is guaranteed for many years and won a *Cat Fancy* magazine Editor's Choice award for Best of Cat Products.

My favorite endorsement of Cat Fence-In comes from Sally Daniels of Ann Arbor who says her cats, Brady and O'Keefe, who "rule the house with iron paws," use their fenced yard to bask in the sun, watch butterflies, and leap about at night chasing lightning bugs. Says Ms. Daniels, "Are they satisfied? Pur-r-fectly!" For a brochure or to dis-

TOP TIP: Teach your cat to walk (happily) on a leash. Take *Cat Fancy* magazine writer Karen Payne's advice: "Don't use a collar, but a sturdy, lightweight figure-eight or figure-H halter with one strap that passes around the cat's neck and another strap that passes around the body behind the forelegs." The harness should fit snugly but shouldn't be *too* tight. Just hook the leash onto the ring in the center above the cat's back and . . . use treats to persuade Kitty Dearest to "come along." At first, just getting used to the harness may take a little while and lots of billing and cooing on your part, but if the harness becomes associated with pleasurable excursions that shouldn't be too long in coming.

cuss options, call or write Cat Fence-In at P.O. Box 795, Sparks, NV 89432 (702-359-4575).

2. Spend time outside with your cat. Smell the roses together. If kitty is young, she may get used to wearing a harness, and as long as you can stand a slow pace, the two or three of you can stroll. One of my cats, Pandora, used to walk along the C & O Canal with me for about a mile, mewing happily all the way. The sight of her surprised our local muskrat family so much that they forgot all fear and came out onto the bank of the adjacent swamp to gawk at her.

The important thing is to be patient and supportive. Don't pull or tug, just go with the flow (or lack thereof!).

3. No matter if you have central air, install a screen on at least one window and provide a cat seat there to allow your cat to smell the great outdoors unless your cat grew up inside, in which case she will think you have lost your mind and are trying to give her pneumonia or poison her with exhaust fumes.

4. Plant indoor grasses for your cat to nibble on. This can be beneficial to her health as well as allow an outdoor fantasy meal. Grass is a natural laxative. The folic acid in the leaves can help Tiddles vomit up those nasty hairballs that make her an embarrassment at parties. Avoid using chemically treated seeds (often identifiable by their clearly dyed green, red, or blue coloring).

You can plant seeds like:

> oats (easy, cheap, big)
> wheat (not wheatgrass)
> Japanese barnyard millet

bluegrass
fescue

Alfalfa and bean sprouts should be used only in small amounts as these may reduce the protein value of other things fed. Those knowledgeable about seeds advise *against* growing or feeding sorghum or Sudan grass to cats as these can cause cyanide poisoning.

TOP TIP: In some areas, like California, where large birds of prey have been known to turn the tables on the feline species by swooping into the yard and snatching a cat or two (or taking chunks of fur for nesting material!), ultraconscientious cat keepers like Maria Peterson of Santa Monica weave a crisscross framework of visible, white string across the top of their yards or other exposed areas to keep kitty safe and in one piece.

15

How Adorable Are You, from Your Cat's Point of View?

There they lie, flat on their backs, legs in the air, eyes tightly closed. Are they dreaming of fish or birds? No. They are dreaming of the perfect you. Whenever those whiskers twitch, they are remembering one of your foibles. Like annoying women who marry a man and then instantly want to reform him, cats have very firm ideas about what they want in a lifetime companion. They can be excused for feeling that way. After all, they didn't choose you, they got stuck with you. Like mail-order brides, if they had hissed and spat and refused to be carried over the threshold, who knows what would have become of them. They might have ended up in the gutter, forced to sell kittens to motorcycle gangs to support their catnip habit.

So, are you your cat's Prince Charming/Cinderella? Or are you a cat's nightmare, a less than ideal guardian and friend, the person who leaves the door open to the nice, warm, cozy dryer and then wonders, too late, what that thumping sound might be? (Don't think this can't happen to you unless you are vigilance itself. Ask Jean Lundy, a devoted shelter reformer and taker-in of animal refugees. One afternoon, as she headed up the basement stairs, having pushed the High-Cottons button, she heard that clumpety-clump sound. Her thought? How grown-up her son was getting to be by actually washing his sneakers! The "sneakers" turned out to be her old tan cat who lost all the skin on his face and feet—and a little part of his mind—that day. Tom made a slow and painful recovery but was never quite the same.)

This checklist allows you to rate your performance from the cat's perspective and to see if you are the cat's pajamas— the conscientious person who has her cat's safety and well-being in mind at all times. I have omitted a few of my favorite "nevers," such as "Never leave the tops off cleaning fluids or leave antifreeze out." I suppose there is as little point to listing that as to saying, "Never back your car into the garage before opening the door." Such things are mistakes. In the case of antifreeze—which, sadly, must smell, to cats, like cod liver oil or some other exotic and alluring delicacy—an encounter is the worst kind of mistake, a fatal error. This deadly liquid turns to aldehyde in cats' bodies, and they die very badly. Dr. Michael Fox, who writes a syndicated column called "The Pet Doctor," reports that cats are also drawn to Clorox. Lids on, please.

I probably should also have listed, "Never toilet train your cat." I know some people swear by such nonsense, but I suspect that they are the same people who insist on torturing ducks and seagulls by throwing bread to a whole flock of them, one minuscule piece at a time. It drives the birds nuts, forces them to exert themselves unnecessarily, makes them wonder at the stupidity of our species, and puts them through paces that serve only to show that the bread-thrower is interested in showing off when all the birds want to do is eat. Not to belabor this point, but because someone is bound to suggest the toilet-training idea, which sounds all very well and good if you don't think about it from the cat's perspective, remember this: Old, very young, tiny, frail, sick, heavy cats, and those who haven't a good sense of balance (not all Welshmen can sing like canaries either!), will not thank you for having to haul their frames, or fail to haul them, up and onto a seat of a shape and at a height designed to accommodate a human being's backside. Well, you've probably grasped my point.

Give yourself one point for every statement that applies:

The Alwayses and the Never-Evers Checklist

1. I have spayed/neutered my cat(s).
2. I never let my cat(s) out unattended (give yourself two points if you have provided an escape-proof yard or other cat exercise area).
3. I always keep the litterbox impeccably clean.
4. I am always on time with meals.
5. I keep a cat carrier and my veterinarian's number handy.
6. My cat(s) can see out of at least one window without having to behave like a contortionist.
7. I know the signs of cystitis.
8. I take time to play with my cat(s) every day, even on

days when I feel bilious, might be fired if I'm late for work (giving you even more time to play with your cat later), or have an important date.

9. I never forget to kiss my cat goodbye when I leave home (give yourself two points if you never leave home—see number eight).

10. I always remember to bring home a present. (This can be as small and inexpensive as a dried leaf or a clod of dirt. The important part is to make an Academy Award–style fuss over the presentation.)

11. I will never smoke in the vicinity of my cat's sensitive nostrils.

12. I give my cat fresh water and scrub out all bowls at least once a day.

13. Number thirteen has proved most unlucky for many a cat who has lost the pads of his feet or her very life to this appliance: I always keep the dryer door closed *and* check for sleeping cats before switching it on.

14. I have provided for my cat in case of my death.

You can take steps to ensure that your cat will be provided for after your death by naming a caretaker for him in your will. Set aside money in a trust fund or make a direct bequest to a trusted caregiver. If you can't find a friend or relative you can rely on, you might ask a local charitable organization with acceptable standards to adopt your animal or to place him in a good home, even to guarantee to euthanize him should this be the best alternative. Make sure you leave the organization enough money to care for your cat if that's what you think best and enough leeway to let him go if pain enters his life.

15. There is a sticker on my front door that reads, IN CASE OF FIRE OR OTHER EMERGENCY, PLEASE RESCUE MY ___ CATS.

16. My cat is always correctly attired in detachable neckwear with a current address and phone number tastefully emblazoned thereupon.

17. I would never be so miserable as to declaw my cat. (If your cat came to you declawed, you can still score a point if you are horrified. Score two points if you have tracked down and tried to educate the perpetrator.)

18. I never board my cat away from my home when I go on vacation (give yourself two points if you never go on vacation).

19. I never send my cat to an outside grooming shop (see chapter 6 for bathing instructions).

20. I never allow the vet to keep my cat overnight. (You may still take a point if the only exception is in the case of extremely serious injury or illness and where the veterinary office is one of those emergency ones that is open and attended all night.) There is no sense in abandoning an already distressed cat to a smelly, strange, usually uncomfortable cage, surrounded by wailing animals and the pungent smell of disinfectant and other patients' feces. You can look after your own cat in your own bedroom and call if there's a problem (far quicker, in all probability, than the night caretaker, if your vet actually bothers to employ one).

21. I would never fly my cat in the cargo hold of a plane.

22. I never make a noise when my cat is trying to rest.

23. I never yell or swear at my cat.

24. I never fail to answer if my cat says something to me.

25. I never throw my cat off the bed or any furniture.

26. I would never give away my cat to someone else (the only excuses here are imprisonment, hospitalization, incapacity, and military dispatch in time of war).

27. I would never leave children, strangers, or people whose reliability I had not verified in charge of my cat.

28. I would never give my cat an aspirin. (Cats cannot metabolize drugs as we can. Aspirin makes them very ill. And just one Tylenol can kill them.)

How Did You Score?

Only your cat is perfect, but any score below 16 out of 29 points on this basic care quiz demands your immediate remedial training. Remember every time you have resolved to eat less fat and then ordered the fries? This is not like that. This is serious business. You must decide immediately to change your stripes. If you don't, your cat will *never* adore you. I'm surprised *you* can live with yourself, for that matter.

This quiz involves some pretty basic pointers on looking after the mental and physical well-being of your cat(s). If you scored 25 or more, I'll be moving in with you. If you scored 20 or less, you simply have to shape up. Where are you failing? What can you do right away to overcome the problem? Put a note on your dashboard? Make an appointment with the vet? Change a plan? Go to some extra effort?

Whatever it takes, if you do it now, you will have become the very person your cat has been sculpting in his sleep. You will, in fact, be the totally adored man or woman of your cat's dreams.

16

Eye of Newt:
What on Earth Is That
in My Cat's Food?

Is feeding a cat complicated? Well, it is and it isn't. But if you think opening a can of cat food is all you have to do to feed your feline, you may have to think again. After reading this chapter, you could well march into your veterinarian's office and rip those pet food pamphlets to shreds. Just as most physicians don't know beans about human nutrition (in fact, only a handful of medical schools even have a course in it!), most vets haven't a clue whether that canned and bagged pet food they recommend has any drawbacks. When I see a vet hand out a free brochure and sample from one of the commercial pet food salespeople and warn their clients away from anything untraditional, I think about the doctors who, thirty years ago, appeared on TV in white coats to advertise cigarettes. It's enough to make your cat's hair stand on end.

Steel yourself. No matter how attractive the ads and labels, commercial cat food is, by and large, muck. Literally, because cows and chickens are fed their own waste (as well as old newspapers, plastic, cement, and other leftovers you wouldn't add to a stew), and figuratively, because pet food comes from animal products (since when is a wing a product?) that end up in the "4-D" bins.

Four-D bins are not where they store the very best copies of 3-D movies. They are the bins into which slaughterhouse workers obediently pitch animal body parts the government inspectors decide are "not fit for human consumption." The four *D*s stand for dead, dying, diseased, and disabled. When you read the words "meat by-products," think of skin, hide, hair, beaks, toes, and tail ends.

Because meat is loaded with E.coli, salmonella, campylobacter, and other tiny forms of virulent bacteria that give people the stomach flu or kill the occasional consumer, and because an impressive four out of five consumers who eat steak and chicken will eventually end up in a soothingly decorated room in the intensive care ward, fighting for their lives after a heart attack, stroke, or cancer, I remain of the opinion that *all* meat should end up in the "unfit for human consumption" bins. Nevertheless, the truly revolting bits, such as lungs with ulcerated tumors on them, and such unsavory "extras" as ear flaps, nose skin, and toe folds (but, hey, save that yummy liver and tongue!) go into the bins.

What else makes up fancy cat food? Sometimes, bits of "recycled" pet cats and dogs who are "rendered," i.e., melted down in processing plants after their bodies are collected from veterinary hospitals and pounds, as well as parts of broken-down racehorses, commonly known as deadstock. And if you think you're missing all that muck when you buy cat food containing "meat meal," think again. Veterinarian

Wendell O. Belfield says, "Do you know what is in meat meal? Urine, fecal matter, hair, pus, meat [from animals afflicted] with cancer and T.B., etc . . . ."

After a big cook-up, all this mess goes into cans or bags with pretty labels, marked "Little Cleopatra," "Veterinarian's Choice," or some other such cute or sciency name. Not only is this "food" revolting, it is expensive. You could pay NASA to name the next space probe after your cat for the amount of money it takes to vittle-up these days.

In the case of commercial cat food, the proof is *not* in the pudding. Cats *will* eat it. After all, they are true carnivores who, given the chance, will rip a mouse's stomach sac out of his belly with as much relish as Caligula relieving his sister of her baby. (Notwithstanding this fact, animals who hunt usually first eat the stomach contents of their prey. Since mice, the cats' favorite staple, are vegetarians, that means cats eat their veggies before they get to the meat portion of the meal.)

There are other things to bear in mind as you contemplate the marketing genius of the pet food–industry person who first figured out that someone would actually pay money for muck.

For starters, R. Geoffrey Broderick, D.V.M., warns, "Every time a pet trustingly eats another bowl of high-sugar pet food, he is being brought that much closer to diabetes, hypoglycemia, overweight, nervousness, cataracts, allergy—and death." It's enough to make you lose your appetite.

The animal feed eaten by the animals who are supposed to be eaten by your cat is also a pesticide potpourri. Cattle are not only *fed* pesticides, but *sprayed* with concentrated doses of them before they go for the happy ride in the nice truck to the slaughterhouse. Pesticides build up in muscle and tissue, i.e., in meats, and are linked to cancer and other nasty and serious health problems in humans, cats, and other animals.

Farm animals, who are, nowadays, granted the privilege of only a brief glimpse of life while incarcerated in tiny cages or stalls, are no longer made of wholesome mother's milk, sunshine, fresh air, and lush pastures. To make sure profits are maximized, most animals unlucky enough to be classed as food are kept indoors for most or all of their lives, fed an artificial diet (see above), injected with drugs, fed hormones, sprayed with chemicals, and so on. All this is to make them put on weight fast, to break down adrenaline produced by the fear and stress they live under, and to attempt to curb the diseases that run rampant through their overcrowded "intensive farming units." What is put into and on them is passed on through their flesh to the consumer. And the most unappetizing, disease-ridden parts are saved for you-know-who. In the case of cat food, the consumer is, of course, your cat.

If you are a vegetarian for ethical reasons, you may have been wondering how you can justify supporting the slaughterhouse. If anyone tells you the pet food market is inconsequential to the meat industry, you can assure them that it is as *consequential* as leather goods—i.e., *very consequential*. Anyone who has priced a pair of leather pumps or a month's supply of canned cat food realizes that there's big money in them thar by-products. When we buy meat pet food we continue to make it economically viable to allow heifers and hens to lie mangled and ignored in their pens and on the ramps to the killing floor. Meat stinks, not just for them, but for cat health, the environment, and all of us.

So do you have to cook for your cat? Well, no, because there are some wholesome processed foods (see list later), and there are certainly lots of "people foods" that cats love; but if you want your cat to adore you for a long, long time, yes, you should make for the kitchen. Cooking for your cat is very loving and thoughtful, as it is for any family member, and good for your cat's health. In fact, I'll include recipes at the end of this chapter that may convince you that, just as you don't have to cook for yourself from scratch, there may be nothing more difficult to this way of life than simply opening a can and mixing a few things together. However, be alert. A cat's dietary needs are different from those of a dog or a human being, so if you are going to take charge of your cat's diet, you must know what essential vitamins and enzymes your cat must have.

For example, the amino acid taurine, which is vital to a cat's growth and well-being, is an excellent case in point. The first cases of taurine deficiency were discovered—not in vegetarian cats—but in cats eating strictly meat-based canned foods! Taurine is destroyed by cooking, it was discovered, so cats who eat cooked meat *must* be fed supplemental, synthetic taurine, just as vegetarian cats are. The only surefire way to avoid having to add synthetic supplements like taurine to cat's food is to feed them raw meats, but this has its own drawbacks, considering the rampant contamination of today's meat supply with such dangerous bacteria as salmonella, campylobacter, trichinosis, and E.coli. However, thanks to the God of Commerce, synthetic taurine supplements are as easy as pie to get. One kind is Seameal, which contains nineteen different types of sea vegetation, taurine, and beta-carotene; twelve vitamins, nineteen minerals, and sixty trace minerals. (See below for sources.)

One cat to point to is Teresa Gibbs's beautiful, black, long-haired cat, Yoko. Yoko has been featured in *The Wall Street Journal,* whose reporter found her tucking into "garbanzo beans, lentils, split peas, and broccoli—with a pinch of garlic." Yoko also "nibbles on asparagus spears" on special occasions. Having met Yoko, I know that she also loves tofu, bean soups, and pasta. Teresa makes sure her beloved cat, whom she adopted from a Washington shelter, gets lots of protein. She also feeds Yoko a supplement called Vegecat that ensures she has enough taurine.

Another ardent "veggie cat" person, Mary Currier, runs a rescue shelter for cat waifs in New Hampshire. She feeds her orphans a strictly vegetarian diet for health and ethical reasons. These lucky strays enjoy cantaloupe (most cats like all sorts of melons), cucumbers, chickpeas, cooked potato, fake hot dogs, and all manner of veggie foods rich in protein and vitamins.

If you try to teach an old cat new cat food tricks, he may do what my cat, Jarvis, did and walk right through the home-cooking I had lovingly prepared for him, not even recognizing it as food! If there is anyone I'd listen to on dealing with this sort of challenge, it is Alisa Mullins, who works at PETA. Alisa advises people new to all this that the way to wean a cat off commercial cat food is to mix a veggie diet in with your cat's regular food and then gradually diminish the amount of commercial food in the mix.

Alisa recommends starting out with veggie burger recipes, because cats seem to universally love them. It is made from wheat gluten and really does taste like meat. Since the mid-

1990s, when veggie Boca Burgers became a White House favorite, not only Boca Burgers, but many other brands have become available in most supermarkets. They can be mashed or crumbled after cooking and used as the basis of other recipes for cats. When Amy Barnes's cat, Rita, discovered veggie fajitas (made from tempeh), she never looked back.

Alisa also recommends sprinkling a little baby food (not the kind with onion powder, which may cause anemia in cats), nutritional (not brewer's) yeast, or even dry catnip on top of a finicky eater's portion. She had to sneak the peas, carrots, and other veggies into one of her cat's food, but reports that fresh, steamed veggies go over better than the canned kind with her cats.

A conscientious cat mom, Alisa adds half a clove of garlic per cat per day, which she mashes in the food processor. She also adds herbs like parsley, sage, and rosemary once in a while, fresh preferably, dried sometimes, and *always* mixes in digestive enzymes, one teaspoon of rosehips powder (a natural source of vitamin C, which helps reduce the chance of cystitis), plus a teaspoon of alfalfa, which is full of vitamins and minerals and a natural diuretic. Phew! The recipes at the end are actually quite simple.

While we're destroying myths about cat food, let's not forget milk. Most cats are actually lactose-intolerant when it comes to trying to digest cows' milk and can get runny stools, upset tummies, and congestion.

Don't forget to look in the Recommended Reading section of this book for more information sources about health and diet, and more recipes, too!

A word about weight control: Be honest. Does your cat

look like a big blimp? A sort of cross between a kitten and a couch? Is your cat a potential challenger to forty-six-pound Himmy, an Australian cat who got so fat he had to be ferried about in a wheelbarrow?

If that's the case, and we all know that Spandex and Stairmasters aren't going to do the trick for her (although the more you play with your cats, the more fat they'll burn off), it's probably time to look at what she's stoking up on. Obesity is a health problem. Cats, like human beings, shorten their life spans when they widen their waistlines. All that fat stressing their hearts and lungs is not a good thing. Dr. Michael Fox, who writes "The Pet Doctor," has good advice to offer. He says, "pet foods are very palatable and low in bulk (fiber), so the animal's appetite is stimulated, but a satisfying feeling of fullness is never achieved." That's why your cats always seem hungry.

Here are Dr. Fox's tips:

1. Never leave dry food overnight.
2. Divide up what they would normally eat at 4 P.M. into three soft-food meals: morning, afternoon, and evening. Do this for a week, then start substituting more and more boiled rice for their regular soft food. Season the rice with a little bouillon. Work up to three parts rice to one part soft food only.

Here's another pointer: Remove food between meals. In nature, cats aren't served cafeteria-style. Their gastric juices have to flow, their adrenaline has to surge, and fasting from one meal to the next means that the energy and the biologi-

TOP TIP: Before cats found their human families, they had to hunt for their supper. All that stalking and pouncing burned off calories. That makes premeal time an ideal time to get that fat cat to stretch a leg or two. Show the can, say the words, but then get your cat used to playing "chase the tin foil ball," "jump for the moon," or some other strenuous game before serving the meal.

cal matter used for digestion are now freed up to do good work in other ways. A fast, even a brief one, helps cleanse the body. Free availability of food can cause a finicky eating syndrome and other things beginning with the letter *f*, i.e., fatness.

VITAL SUPPLEMENTS

Vegepet products are made by a company committed to *closing* slaughterhouses and providing cats (and dogs) with pure food. You can prepare the meals they suggest in your own kitchen once a week using the sort of ingredients, such as garbanzo beans, gluten flour, and yeast, that you can pick up at any health food store. Once you've made the slop, you just add Vegecat powder, and you'll meet your cat's full nutritional needs.

Vegepet does provide kibble recipes for an extra measure of convenience, and my cats love the stuff. The methods are outlined in detailed instructions accompanying each container of supplement; it takes about thirty minutes to make ten days' worth of kibble. Other recipes are even shorter.

Kittens up to twelve months old require *Vegekit*. If you have both kittens and older cats, you can feed them all *Vegekit*. *Vegecat* does seem to make cats' coats shine, and because there is no rotting meat in any of the food, an added bonus is less smelly cat feces—something we all appreciate more than one can put into words.

Vegecat prices are: $7.50 for an eight-week supply, $15.00 for a four-and-a-half month supply, and $27.00 for a nine-month supply. You can contact the Vegepet people at 717 East Missoula Avenue, Troy, MT 59935-9609 (800-884-6262).

VegeYeast is a powdered supplement made from nutritional yeast and is specially processed and pH-adjusted for finicky cats, which means 80 percent of all cats alive at any given time. Because cats have a preference for acid products, and because of the importance of keeping urine acidic, this product makes a good choice. It can be used in all of the Vegekit recipes. Dogs like it, too.

The prices per pound are: 1/$4.25, 2/$4.00–$8.00, 3/$3.75–$11.25, 5/$3.60–$18.00, and 10/$3.50–$35.00.

Commercial Cat Food:

Evolution—vegan cat kibble
815 South Robert Street.
St. Paul, MN 55107
Wysong Corporation—vegan cat kibble

1880 North Eastman Road
Midland, MI 48640
1-800-748-0188

HOME COOKING FOR
THE CAT YOU LOVE: RECIPES

Kittens (up to eight to twelve months old) have mineral and vitamin requirements different from adult maintenance and need Vegekit. For cats prone to Feline Urologic Syndrome (FUS), avoid whole grains and try adding 500 mg of ascorbic acid (vitamin C) per day to meals. It can help prevent infection and acidify the urine. Seitan, gluten flour, seaweed vegetables, yeast, and soy (use tofu coagulated with calcium sulfate, not nigari, for low magnesium) can all be found in natural food stores. Choose oils from the following group: olive, high oleic (not regular) safflower, canola (rapeseed), peanut, sunflower, or sesame.

VEGEKIBBLE
This is my favorite recipe for convenience and palatability. It's very flexible since many coatings are possible for flavor variations and most cats take to it well. Once the routine of making kibble is established, you'll find it easy and well worth the initial learning stage.

60 DAYS FOOD
(SAVE TIME BY STORING PREMIXED DRY INGREDIENTS FOR LATER USE.)

15 cups gluten flour
5 cups corn meal
4 ¼ cups wheat germ
3 cups defatted soy flour (3 ½ cups if whole)
3 ¾ cups yeast powder
1 ⅓ cups Vegecat
⅔ cup nonaluminum baking powder (optional: this makes a lighter kibble)
Optional: garlic powder or tomato paste
2 tablespoons salt (see below)

Salt may be left out of the dry mixture, and replaced by 2 tablespoons soy or tamari sauce when making the regular 13-day food recipe. A gallon food pail makes a good shaker and storage for dry ingredients. If baking 60 days food (nine cookie sheets' worth) all at once, you would also add:

2 1/4 cups oil
Water necessary to form dough

REGULAR 13-DAY VEGEKIBBLE

1 cup corn flour
⅔ cup defatted soy flour (1 cup if whole)
3 ¼ cups gluten flour
⅞ cup wheat germ

¾ *cup yeast powder*
⅓ *cup Vegecat*
⅛ *cup baking powder*
½ *tablespoons salt (if not added before) or 1/8 cup soy or*
tamari sauce
½ *cup oil*
Small can tomato paste (optional)
3 cups water or broth (as necessary)

Preheat oven to 325°F (160°C)

Add ½ cup oil and 3 cups water (as necessary) to 7 cups of the 60-Day dry ingredient mixture. If you aren't storing pre-mixed dry ingredients for later use, start with the measurements for 13 days.

Flour your hands and counter and knead into a pie crust–like dough. Taking one half of the dough, roll out to about ¼"–⅜" thickness to fit a large cookie sheet. Place on cookie sheet and roll out the other half of the dough like the first. Place sheets on oven upper racks and bake at 325°F for 20 minutes.

Remove from oven. Flip half-baked kibble over by putting another (third) cookie sheet on top, holding both together, and carefully turning over. Do the same to the other sheet.

Bake for 20 minutes more. Remove from the oven, cool slightly. Using a large slightly curved knife, cut each sheet into 12 parts on a cutting board. First cut horizontally into three strips, and then cut each of those strips into fourths. Cut each resulting square into kibble-size pieces (like a miniature checker board) by cutting first in one direction, and then cutting all those little strips in the other direction.

Place kibble in a warm oven (about 200°F) for 2 to 3 hours until crunchy dry. Sunshine or food dehydrators are good dryers.

Store in covered container. Refrigeration isn't necessary.

Garbanzo Soy 10 Days Food

4 ½ cups canned garbanzo beans
1 ⅓ cups crumbled veggie burger or 2 cups tofu
⅞ cup yeast powder
⅓ cup oil
1 teaspoon salt or 4 teaspoons soy sauce
¼ cup Vegecat
Seasonings

Soak garbanzo beans in cool water until double in size. Change soak water if necessary to keep beans from fermenting. Drain, cover with fresh water, and cook until just soft.

Drain thoroughly and crush warm beans with a potato masher. Food processors can crush cold beans. Stir in the other ingredients, letting the mixture soften before serving.

Coat bite-size chunks with yeast.

Lentil Soy 10 Days Food

1 ¾ cups uncooked lentils
1 ⅚ cups textured vegetable protein
¾ cup yeast powder
⅜ cup oil

1 teaspoon salt or 4 teaspoons soy sauce
¼ cup Vegecat
Seasonings

Soak lentils in cold water for two hours. Drain, cover with water, and cook until just soft. Thoroughly drain and add other ingredients. Let the textured vegetable protein soften in the mixture before serving. Coat with yeast prior to serving.

RICE/OAT SOY 12 DAYS FOOD

1 ¾ cups uncooked parboiled rice or
8 ⅛ cups cooked quick oats
2 ⅓ cups textured vegetable protein or 3 ⅔ cups firm tofu
1 cup yeast powder
7 tablespoons oil
4 ½ tablespoons Vegecat
1 ¼ teaspoons salt or 5 teaspoons soy sauce
Seasonings (garlic powder, etc.)

You can entice even the finickiest cat with "Sprinkles," a 100 percent vegetarian blend of "proprietary yeasts" used as a flavor enhancer. Sprinkles comes in a salt shaker and all you do is sprinkle it on. Available from Nickerson International, 12 Schubert Street, Staten Island, NY 10305 (1-800-NICKERS), at about $6 postpaid.

17

Saying It with Flowers: Holistic Remedies

Some plants hurt, others heal. That's the difference between "flower remedies," the relatively new application of the oldest medicines and pick-me-ups in history, borne of forest lore, and plants that use their natural defenses, like poisons secreted from their leaves, to ward off attacks by cats and other marauding nonplants.

THE CURATIVE POWER OF FLOWERS

Cats need not only smell the roses, they can eat them, too.

Two English friends, Hilly Beavan and Anthony Lawrence, never leave home without a bottle of "Bach's Rescue Remedy," a mixture of flowers, including impatiens and clematis, that produce calming, stabilizing effects when cats and other animals experience stress.

More "rat people" than "cat people," Hilly and Ant have been heavily romanced by two white Norway rats who took refuge in their home after the traumas of laboratory life. They gained respect for the contents of Bach's little bottle when they saw its effect in helping the rats "get normal again." They have since tried it on larger whiskered beings and swear that, whatever the incident or accident, you should always bring out the Bach's.

"It works," says Hilly, "for just about anything, including a run-in with a collie or a car, for insect bites and cat fights, trips to the vet, and just about anything ugly that could befall a poor cat."

Bach's "Original Flower Remedies" were first composed in 1930 by Dr. Edward Bach, an English physician who found that if patient stress is left unresolved it inevitably leads to physical disorder. Dr. Bach put together thirty-eight remedies that were not only harmless (harsh drugs are not among the ingredients), but safe, gentle, and, many believe, very effective.

The many testimonials in *Flowers to the Rescue* (see Recommended Reading) echo Hilly and Ant's experience. For example, G. S. Khalsa, a Michigan physician, writes, "I was visiting a veterinarian friend of mine when another friend brought in a cat who appeared to be quite exhausted. The cat had been out in the rain all day and was frightened. We gave him one dose of Rescue Remedy and, within five minutes, the cat was purring, cozy, and friendly." No wonder some people take a little dose at the end of a work day from hell.

A few drops in a teaspoon of water, drizzled onto the tongue or popped into drinking water, and a traumatized cat feels more sedate and able to cope with what life may offer next.

Bach's remedies aren't only for major traumas. If you have a cat who is jealous, irritable, afraid, or dealing with a distressing experience, such as a household move, travel sickness, or a new baby in the family, there may be a flower remedy that will help.

Among the remedies most recommended for cats are these:

Clematis. Anytime a cat appears stunned or experiences unusual patterns of sleeping beyond the typical catnap. Used in helping regain consciousness after an accident or operation.

Chicory. Helps stabilize the emotions of an extremely jealous cat. This is a very helpful remedy when you are trying to introduce another cat into the family and your cat has turned green.

Beech. For the cat who has no tolerance for other animals or certain people. A great icebreaker that came in handy in the case of a diplomat's Siamese who used to hide under the couch and then bite into visiting dignitaries' ankles. It is used with *Walnut* to assist in keeping the peace between two cats who are always at each other's throats.

Mimulus. Helps cats overcome fear of thunderstorms; Wagnerian music; vacuum cleaners; trips to the vet; the encroachment of screaming, small children; and other particular worries.

Aspen. If a cat slinks from place to place out of fear, never at complete ease, startling at sounds. (If you suspect past human-caused abuse, *Star of Bethlehem* is recommended. If you suspect current human-caused abuse, call the humane society.)

Larch. Can help the lowest-ranking cat, the runt, for example, gain self-confidence and become more emotionally balanced.

Star of Bethlehem. For all trauma, past and present, physical and psychological. For recuperation from surgery, injury, boarding, and other nasty occurrences that affect a cat's dignity, freedom, health, or security.

Honeysuckle. It's not only "hep cats" who get the blues. This remedy can be helpful for a grieving cat who has lost someone close to him/her and feels depressed and alone.

Calming Essence. For car trips, accidents, illness, injury, during a long absence, before and after surgery, any extreme stress.

Among homeopathic treatments I have heard particularly promising reports on are those used for arthritis (Arth-Ease), for example, and for relief from itching and allergies (Aller-Ease). Both are available from Ellon USA, Inc., 644 Merrick Road, Lynbrook, NY 11563.

Take a look in the Recommended Reading and Handy Resources sections of this book for information on other companies, such as Anaflora, a company that provides twenty-six flower essence formulas that address the "physical, mental, emotional, and spiritual needs" of animals and will send a free brochure on their products. They can be reached at P.O. Box 1056, Mt. Shasta, CA 96067 (916-926-6424).

HERBS AND HOMEOPATHY

Veterinarians who practiced homeopathy used to be as scarce as hens' teeth. Now they're not very hard to find.

Most not only use plant extracts or herbal medicine to try to cure what ails a cat, where such treatment is considered appropriate, but look at other methods that take into consideration the whole cat.

Such veterinarians, many of whom join the American Holistic Veterinary Medical Association, find that homeopathic treatments can sometimes do the job where conventional veterinary medicine (allopathy) has failed, and at other times such methods work well in tandem with traditional medicine. For example, Dr. Richard Pitcairn, who is considered to be the leading homeopathic veterinarian in the United States, advises cat owners to use *symphytum* to help heal fractures. It is made from the comfrey plant and used to be called "knit-bone" long, long ago—a dead giveaway that it is believed to aid healing.

If you go to a homeopathic vet, don't be surprised to hear questions about your cat's preferences for a sleeping place, how he relates to others of all species in the household, and sundry oddball questions the answers to which may give important clues as to what is going on mentally and physically.

Some homeopaths use other alternative techniques, now routinely available to human patients, such as acupuncture (which can be wonderful for joint pain), Chinese herbal medicine, and chiropractic. I'll let Ulla Davis's story about her cat, Cuchuma, tell the tale:

Cuchuma was taking high doses of cortisone and painkillers because of trouble with his back. An otherwise healthy ten-year-old, Cuchuma could no longer get up onto Davis's lap, something which caused both cat and human great sadness.

Davis took her cat to Dr. Raymond Deiter, a holistic veterinarian in Sausalito, for an acupuncture treatment. "At the first treatment, he didn't do anything when the doctor put the needles in," Davis told Melinda Sacks of the *San Jose Mercury News*. "He just put his little face on my arm and went to sleep."

Cuchuma had five treatments over a five-week period and can now get up and down from his bed easily.

PLANT GOT YOUR CAT'S TONGUE?

Some of our most popular house plants are poisonous and can do quite a bit of damage to an unsuspecting cat. I recommend an inventory of the household greenery you have at hand and a quick check when you consider buying a new plant.

Luckily, most cats don't seem to feel the urge to chew on North America's favorite hanging, dangling plant, the *philodendron*. Even if you are not a heart surgeon, you will be able to recognize the shape of the leaves on this plant, which is also known as heart-leaf because no one sat up all night thinking of something more complicated to call it. The leaves may look cute and romantic, but like Mata Hari, they will betray you: Inside, they contain needlelike crystals of poisonous acid.

Should a cat sink her teeth into a philodendron, the acid mixes with her saliva and makes her mouth, throat, and tongue burn like a chili dinner. Jack, one of the PETA cats, found this out the hard way, having discovered a philodendron left as a gift for the hardworking staff in our Research and Investigation department. His screams were enough to get the whole fourth floor running to his aid. Jack subsequently lost all interest in horticulture, and the plant was whisked away forever.

Another popular plant is the *dieffenbachia*, or mother-in-law plant, which has large, oblong leaves painted with light white splotches. This, too, contains acid that causes burning and can make a cat's tongue and throat swollen and terribly painful. If the tongue swells too much, it can block the cat's throat and cause suffocation, necessitating an emergency run to the vet. Sap from the dieffenbachia can cause eye problems, such as inflammation.

Hydrangia is bad, too. It comes in bushes, large and small, and has very pretty clusters of blue, white, or pink flowers. It can cause stomach cramps, gastrointestinal disturbance, bloody diarrhea, problems of the heart, lungs, and kidneys.

Forget *Caladium*, with its flashy, bright, heart-shaped leaves in combinations of green, white, orange, and red. It causes burning and pain to the tongue, throat, and mouth. Again, suffocation is possible should the cat's tongue swell to block his throat.

And most *Ivy* is out. As attractive as these climbing plants are with their petite leaves, often green-flecked or edged with white, the small berries on many varieties are extremely dangerous and cause inflammation of the throat and stomach, if swallowed.

Also on the "don't bring home or the cat gets it" list are:

amaryllis	Jerusalem cherry
arrowhead vine	marble queen
asparagus fern	mistletoe
azalea	pot mum

bird of paradise
Boston ivy
cherry
chrysanthemum
creeping charlie
creeping fig
daffodil
elephant ears
emerald duke
english holly

iris
red princess
rubber plants
schefflera
spider mum
spider plant
sprengeri fern
tulip
weeping fig

Phew! (That's not a plant, just an expression.)

WHAT TO DO IN A POISONING EMERGENCY

Call the National Animal Poisoning Information Network at The College of Veterinary Medicine at The University of Illinoise in Urbana at 800-548-2423 to speak to a veterinarian.

Get your cat to a vet by kit helicopter, fast car, or however you can. If you are in a cabin in the woods and have a flat tire during a blizzard, Darlene Polachic, a writer for *Cat Fancy* magazine, advises this:

If your cat has *not* eaten a plant that causes throat irritation, try to get your cat to vomit. Fill a syringe or baster with one of the following:

- lukewarm soapy water, hydrogen peroxide mixed with an equal amount of lukewarm water, one teaspoon of salt dissolved in a cup of water, *or*
- one teaspoon of mustard powder mixed with a cup of lukewarm water.

TOP TIP: There's no need to go plantless. Ms. Polachic also points out that cats can have a little chew on the following plants, *without* causing you heart failure:

> begonias
> coleus
> spleenwort
>   (Don't you hope it tastes better than it
>   sounds?)
> ti plant
> wandering Jew
> prayer plant
> dracaena
> Succulents,
>   like jade plant, donkey tail, and coral beads

Squirt the solution down the cat's throat.

Next, try to bind the poison to slow its absorption. Feed the cat a mixture of vegetable oil, milk (soy or any kind), egg whites if you have them. Follow the treatment with a laxative or warm-water enema.

This does not sound like a fun way to spend even five minutes. Removing even the prettiest of poisonous plants to solve the problem before it happens seems a far better idea.

And the latest news about poinsettia, once thought to be poisonous, is that it isn't. Sadly, I must inform my cats that the news on chocolate is that it still is, for cats.

HOLISTIC VETERINARY RESOURCES

The International Veterinary Acupuncture Society
Certified in veterinary acupuncture.
Box 142, the Mail Station
1750-1 30th Street
Boulder, CO 80301

American Veterinary Chiropractic Association
Certified in veterinary chiropractic care.
P.O. Box 249
Port Byron, IL 61275

Animal Natural Health Center
Certified in veterinary homeopathy.
1283 Lincoln Street
Eugene, OR 97410

American Holistic Veterinary Medical Association
Oriented toward holistic animal healthcare.
2214 Old Emmorton Road
Bel Air, MD 21015
Tel: 410-569-0795
Fax: 410-569-2346

International Veterinary Acupuncture Society
2140 Conestoga Road
Chester Springs, PA 19425

Dr. Richard H. Pitcairn
His helpful courses are for the public as well as for veterinarians and take place in the spring.
1283 Lincoln Street
Eugene, OR 97401

The National Center for Homeopathy
801 North Fairfax Street, Suite 306
Alexandria, VA 22314

The International Foundation for Homeopathy
2366 East Lake Avenue East, Suite 301
Seattle, WA 98102

Animal Connection (a web site only)
Holistic Health for Animals
http://www.cyberark.com/animal/holistic.htm

Homeopathic First Aid for Pets (video)
Video Remedies
P.O. Box 290866
Davie, FL 33329
(1-800-733-4874)

Recommended Charities

ALLEY ANIMALS

Get out the tissues if you dare read this marvelous group's newsletter. Local to Baltimore, Maryland, this plucky band of volunteers plys the endless labyrinth of alleyways, abandoned houses, and drug-dealer hangouts, rescuing those poor animals society has truly cast out. Sometimes, they are too late, as with "Little Innocent One," excerpted here from the Alley Animals news bulletin.

The night started off quietly for us as we began our route through the alleys (although the night is never quiet or peaceful for the animals struggling to survive there). But I was about to be taken by a whirlwind of emotion when I pulled into an alleyway and saw a kitten lying on the cement in front of the car. I said to myself, "My God, I hope she's still alive." I jumped out to retrieve her.

Before I picked her up I knew she was dead, but she had not been so for long, the blood from her limp body on my hands, still moist. As I carried her body back to the car, I could hardly contain my anger. I wanted to shout out, "Who did this! Where are you hiding? Come out to face me and the crime you committed against this innocent one. Come out from hiding, coward."

I could plainly see all the "fun" that was had in the wicked ugly things done to her. She had to have been friendly to allow herself to be handled—a wild kitten instinctively knows not to trust humans. All she hoped for was a little kindness, maybe something to eat. Instead, she was hung with a clothesline and, the many jagged rips in her skin told me, thrown to the dogs.

I could only imagine what she had gone through, a friendly kitten trusting the wrong person who repaid this act of innocence by torturing her unspeakably. I want you to look at her and remember that this is why we are fighting so hard to get these animals off the streets.

All donations are gratefully received and put to good use. Alley Animals, P.O. Box 27487, Towson, MD 21285-7487.

THE GREEK CAT WELFARE SOCIETY

Brought together by an Englishwoman, Christine Morison, their veterinarians visit the islands of Greece, and a group in Athens goes to the National Gardens every day to care for the endless stream of homeless kitties who congregate there, hoping for a handout. They can be contacted through the Greek Animal Welfare Fund, Ltd., 1-2 Castle Lane, London SW1E 6DR, or you can contact the Greek Cat Welfare Society directly via fax: 30-1-725-8497.

PEOPLE FOR THE ETHICAL TREATMENT OF ANIMALS

501 Front Street
Norfolk, VA 23510
Tel: 757-622-7382
Fax: 757-622-0457

PETA is an international nonprofit animal protection organization dedicated to establishing and defending the rights of all animals. With 600,000 members worldwide, PETA works through public education, research and investigations, grassroots organizing, and media campaigns to expose and eliminate animal abuse wherever it occurs.

ROMAN ASSOCIATION FOR THE PROTECTION OF ANIMALS

ARCA
Viale delle Medaglie d'Oro, 165
Roma, Italy

This group runs a shelter in the shadow of the Torre Argentina in Rome, the archaeological site where Julius Caesar was assassinated by Brutus. They capture the hundreds of abandoned, lame, blind, nursing, sick, and aged cats deposited at the site by their uncaring owners and try to stop the population from growing beyond all bounds.

Their desperate current need is to raise funds to connect their little shelter to the main sewer system and to install proper drains to allow them to clean the cat runs more efficiently.

BEST FRIENDS ANIMAL SANCTUARY

Best Friends is home to domestic animals who were once homeless, abused, or neglected and also to a host of wildlife who find sanctuary there. They operate a low-cost spay/neuter program and sponsor a national network of animal lovers in animal rescue, foster care, and humane education. You can contact them at Best Friends Animal Sanctuary, Kanab, UT 84741-5001, (tel) 801-644-2001, (fax) 801-644-5848, or E-mail: animalnet@msn.com.

SUPPORT YOUR LOCAL SHELTER

Please consider helping the wonderful people who rescue, adopt, shelter, re-home, and euthanize your local cast-off animals. Their work is hard, thankless, and never-ending.

Recommended Reading

BOOKS

Bamberger, Michelle, DVM. *HELP! The Quick Guide to First Aid for Your Cat.* MacMillan Publishing, Howell Book House, 201 W. 103rd St., Indianapolis, IN 46290, 1-800-858-7674.
Written by a veterinarian, this is a very useful, quick-reference book you would like to be able to put your hands on in a cat emergency.

Barish, Eileen. *Doin' Arizona and Doin' California, Travels with a Cat or Dog.* Pet Friendly Publications, P.O. Box 8459, Scottsdale, AZ 85252.

Barish, Eileen. *Eileen's Directory of Pet Friendly Lodging.* Pet Friendly Publications, P.O. Box 8459, Scottsdale, AZ 85252.

Busch, Heather, and Burton Silver. *Why Cats Paint: A Theory of Feline Aesthetics.* (1994, $14.95) Ten Speed Press, P.O. Box 7123, Berkeley, CA 94707, 1-800-841-BOOK.
This isn't useful in any way, but it is very funny and exquisitely done, so I had to include it. If you feel down in the dumps or need a special present for an arty friend who cares about cats, this is it.

Callahan, Sharon. *Flower Essence Therapy for Animals.* P.O. Box 1056, Mt. Shasta, CA 96067, 916-926-6424.

Carlson, Delbert G., D.V.M., and James M. Griffin, M.D. *Cat Owner's Home Veterinary Handbook.* New York: Howell Book House, 1995.
Recommended as a medical reference only. The term "cat owner" accurately sums up the authors' disregard for cats' individuality and sentience. But as a nonhomeopathic, nonholistic medical reference, the book is comprehensive and user-friendly.

Fox, Dr. Michael W. *The Healing Touch.* New York: Newmarket Press, 1990.
Easy to follow directions, useful photos, strong medical rationale (Fox explains techniques based on both homeopathic and allopathic interpretation).

Frazier, Anitra, with Norma Eckroate. *The New Natural Cat: A Complete Guide for Finicky Owners.* New York: Plume, 1990.
*Very comprehensive, damns declawing, pro–raw foods diet, regards the cat as a sentient being, unlike some books that regard them as machines to be maintained . . . **BUT!** . . . her nutrition information is out of date since the emergence of Vegecat.*

Hine, Muriel. *Simply Precious—Moments in Time with a Remarkable Cat.*
Send $12.95 + $3.95 shipping and handling to Precious, Department 6, 1075 Watervliet Shaker Rd., Albany, NY 12205. Proceeds benefit Best Friends Sanctuary. The engaging story of a much loved cat and her impact on family and friends.

Hunter, F. *Homeopathic First-Aid Treatment for Pets.* New York: Thorsons Publishers, Inc., 1984/1988.

McHattie, Grace. *Your Cat Naturally.* New York: Carroll & Graf Publishers, 1992.
Another informative book that is unfortunately not quite current nutritionally. She's also inclined to let a cat outside unattended. I recommend this book for its impressive charts of homeopathic and herbal remedies for a number of ailments, as well as its thorough approach to cat care (meat diet notwithstanding).

Maggitti, Phil. *Guide to a Well-Behaved Cat.* Barron's Educational Series, 250 Wireless Blvd., Hauppauge, NY 11788, 1-516-434-3311.
Written by a kind person with a wonderful sense of what animals need, this book contains great tips on how to patiently and gently train a cat to walk on a lead.

Peden, James A. *Vegetarian Cats and Dogs.* Troy, MT: Harbingers of a New Age, 1995.
Formidable amount of scientific/clinical information, yet easy to read. A useful, comprehensive sourcebook for antimeat and pro—raw foods feline diet.

The Doctor's Book of Home Remedies for Dogs and Cats, Ed. *Prevention Magazine* Health Books. New York: Bantam, 1991.
This reference manual lists over 1,000 remedies, and each chapter has a special feature called "When to See the Vet," which should always be read first.

Plechner, A., and M. Zucker. *Pet Allergies, Remedies for an Epidemic.* Inglewood, CA: Very Healthy Enterprises, 1986.

Progressive Animal Welfare Society (PAWS). *The Hands-on Handbook.* Seattle: Progressive Animal Welfare Society, 1995.
Cheap and contains helpful hints, including how to trap a frightened or feral (wild) cat, what to do to rescue a cat stuck in a tree, plus tips on cat laws and useful information about animal shelters.

Reed, John Avalon. *The Whole Kitty Catalog.* Crown Trade Paperbacks, 201 E. 50th St., New York, NY 10022.
This fantastic book helps you select hundreds of toys for your cat (and a few items you or your cat-friendly friends might personally enjoy).

Rhea, Alice. *Good Cats, Bad Habits.* New York: Fireside, 1995.
Easy to use, quick-reference guide covering a wide range of topics. Alphabetical listings. Uses effective Q & A format. She denounces declawing and letting cats roam freely.

Stein, Diane. *Natural Healing for Dogs & Cats.* Freedom, CA: The Crossing Press, 1993.

Designed for human companions who want a very nontraditional approach to animal care. Large sections devoted to psychic healing and reincarnation, which may prove too New Age to some (these sections are useful to everybody, however, in establishing attitudes about death, coping with grief, and reaffirming spirituality of individual animals).

Vlamis, Gregory. *Flowers to the Rescue, The Healing Vision of Dr. Edward Bach.* New York: Thorsons, 1986.

Walker, Bob. *The Cats' House.* Kansas City, MO: Andrew & Meel, 1996.
The absolute end in how to design your house to suit the cats. And good ideas for humbler plans.

Wilbourn, Carole, C. *The Cat Caring Tape.*
The author of this respect-filled and sensitive audiotape claims that her voice soothes and calms troubled cats. The tape is useful for any human involved with a cat. She theorizes that many quirky and awful behavioral characteristics are brought on by a cat's low self-esteem and offers ideas on how to build up kitty's psyche (and one's own) for a mutually rewarding and enjoyable experience.

Wolf, H. *Your Healthy Cat.* Berkeley, CA: Homeopathic Educational Services, 1991.

Wright, John C. *Is Your Cat Crazy.* Macmillan Publishing Company, 201 W. 103rd St., Indianapolis, IN 46290, 1-800-428-5331, $18.
Written by a cat therapist, this book contains some helpful sug-

gestions to help bewildered people seek the root of cat behavior problems.

The Doctors Book of Home Remedies for Dogs and Cats and a booklet *Why Does My Cat Do That?* are available from Rodale Books, (Tel.) 1-800-848-4735 or (Fax) 1-800-813-6627.

MAGAZINES

Cat Fancy
P.O. Box 6050
Mission Viejo, CA 92690-6050
714-855-8822.
Editorial material delves into all aspects of cat care ranging from nutritional ideas to tips for choosing the correct cat toys.

Cats Magazine
2 News Plaza
Peoria, Il 61614
1-800-521-2885
Features include veterinarian and behavior advice, new products, and book reviews.

I Love Cats
950 Third Ave.
16th Floor, New York, NY 10022-2705
Features news and information for cat owners, including nutrition, veterinary advice, homeopathic remedies, as well as stories about cat lovers and adventures.

Vegepet Gazette,
717 E. Missoula Ave.
Troy, MT 59935-9609
800-884-6262
The Vegepet Gazette *is a twelve- to sixteen-page newsletter that includes the latest information on pet nutrition. It contains stories and pictures of experiences with Vegepet products. A subscription brings you four valuable issues.*

Cat Faeries Catalog
3964 26th St.
Department BF, San Francisco
CA 94131
Organic catnip, catnip massage oil, and all sorts of things for cataholics, such as T-shirts and books on feline mysticism.

FOR CHILDREN

Crimmins, C. E., ed. The Quotable Cat. Philadelphia: Running Press, 1992.
This is a fun book, absolutely chock-full of sayings, mostly pro-cat, of all sorts of people, many recognizable, some not.

Markham, Ann. *The Cat with a Black Ring.* New York: Vantage, 1996.
The delightful story of a cat who is abandoned and finds a home. It introduces children gently to the idea that cats are not always well treated and that some need our help.

Newkirk, Ingrid. *Kids Can Save the Animals! 101 Easy Things to Do*. New York: Warner Books, 1991.
This book gives kids facts about animals, animal-friendly companies, and over one hundred projects and ideas that show how they can help save all creatures great and small.

World Wide Web Sites

Pet Talk—Frequently Asked Questions
www.zmall.com/pet talk/cat-faqs/general-care.html

PETA Online
www.envirolink.org/arrs/peta/index.html

The Cat Fanciers' Association
www.cfainc.org/cfa/

HandiLinks to Cats
www.ahandyguide.com/cat1/c/c764.htm

The Traditional Cat Association
www.covesoft.com/tca/

Handy Resources

CAT SAFETY

Blinking Safety Light Tag, $12. Visible for 2,000 feet, long-lasting battery, clip-on. From: Pet Friendly Publications, P.O. Box 8459, Scottsdale, AZ 85252, 1-800-638-3637.

The Feline Safety Curtain helps prevent garage door tragedies. It is billed as "100% effective." For information call 713-271-8414 or send a self-addressed stamped envelope to P.O. Box 2692, Bellaire, TX 77402-2692.

Cat seat belts are available from Omaha Vaccine Pet Catalog, 3030 L St., Omaha, NE 68107, 1-800-367-4444. About $20, plus shipping.

CAT HEALTH

Melia's Kitty Greens Garden. This includes a hand painted terra cotta pot and a box of soil and seeds. You just add water. For a free catalog write to 2103 N. Decatur Rd., Suite 222, Atlanta, GA 30033, or call 404-315-6377.

Feline First-Aid Kit. This contains all the basics, including scissors, bandages, burn ointment—everything you can't find when you need it. Very handy for carrying in the car. The company sends a free pocket/travel kit for human use with every feline kit ordered. Free information: Outdoor Safety, P.O. Box 103-CM, Winona, MN 55987.

Feline Massage Workshops. Not a book, but a course. The workshops are designed to promote health and wellness for cats of all ages and sizes and are taught by licensed massage therapists. For a free brochure, call 1-800-251-0007.

T-Touch Cats and Kittens from Thane Marketing International, 78080 Calle Estado, 2nd Floor, La Quinta, CA 92253, 1-760-777-0217 is Linda Tellington-Jones's method of calming and soothing distressed cats and trying to correct objectionable behaviors that may be caused by a cat's stress or insecurity.

Natural Light. If you absolutely can't make any outdoor arrangements, you might install full-spectrum natural lighting in at least one favorite cat room in your home. Some power companies offer discounts to consumers who swap standard strip lighting for these bulbs. Natural lights are also available for desk and reading lights as well as for overhead bulbs. Contact Valentine, Inc., 4259 S. Western Blvd., Chicago, IL 60609, 1-800-GET-STUF.

DEALING WITH GRIEF

Intense feelings of grief over the death of a loved one are a normal and natural experience. Should it matter whether the loved one is a human being or a cherished companion animal? Grief counselor Charlene Douglas doesn't think so, and she's right. Charlene is assistant director of the People-Pet Partnership at Washington State University's College of Veterinary Medicine. She offers her professional services, at no cost, via the Internet. She can also send you helpful information in a grief support package.

Contact her at People-Pet Partnership, College of Veterinary Medicine, Washington State University, P.O. Box 647010, Pullman, WA 99164-7010, 509-335-4569 or by E-mail at douglasc@wsu,edu.

CAT ENTERTAINMENT

Cat Walk Plans. For cats to run high up, alongside the walls, just under the ceiling, or sleep and hang out safely from above. For a photo, list of supplies, and clear plans send $15 to Pet Projects-CM, Chester, MA 01011-0623.

Custom-made tunnels can be had for the adventurous or reclusive cat. Made of rope and anchored by supports, they are sold to your specs by linear foot. Contact House of Cats International, 25011 Bell Mountain Dr., San Antonio, TX 78255, 1-800-889-7402.

A ramp in need is a friend indeed, especially to arthritic cats or others with trouble getting about. Pet Care with Love, P.O. Box 764, Glenview, IL 60025, 1-800-441-1765 sells adjustable ramps in small, medium, and large that can help kitty maneuver up the couch.

You can even get ready-made stairs. The Kitty Walk attaches to just about any surface and lets your cat stride or stroll up to whatever perch you've chosen. Available from Avcon Products, 10162 Orangewood Ave., Garden Grove, CA 92640.

The very best cat tree in the world is from The Jellicle Cat Company (9311 NW 26th Place, Sunrise, FL 33322, 1-954-748-0698) and comes with tunnels, tubes, viewing platforms, and nest boxes. It costs about $430, plus freight.

Stain Remover

Nature's Miracle Stain and Odor Remover. Pets 'N People, 930 Indian Peak Rd., Ste. 215, Rolling Hills Estates, CA 90274, 310-544-7125.

Other Ways to Help the Animals

Animal-Friendly Checks. This idea is catching on. Why use a boring bank check when you can make a difference for the animals every time you pay a bill! Checks with cat prints and other animal-y designs are available from the following charities who use the profit from sales of the checks to fund their work.

Hawaiian Humane Society Checks
Community Check
P.O. Box 43833
Baltimore, MD 21236

PETA Checks
Message!Check
P.O. Box 64800
St. Paul, MN 55164-0800

Index